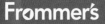

Frommer's

London
day BY day®
6th Edition

T0102192

by Donald Strachan

FrommerMedia LLC

Contents

Published by:

Frommer Media LLC

Copyright © 2024 FrommerMedia LLC, New York, NY. All rights reserved. No part of this publication may be reproduced, stored in a retrieval system or transmitted in any form or by any means, electronic, mechanical, photocopying, recording, scanning or otherwise, except as permitted under Sections 107 or 108 of the 1976 United States Copyright Act, without the prior written permission of the Publisher. Requests to the Publisher for permission should be addressed to Support@FrommerMedia.com.

ISBN: 978-1-628-87595-9 (paper); 978-1-628-87596-6 (ebk)
Editorial Director: Pauline Frommer
Editor: Pauline Frommer
Production Editor: Heather Wilcox
Photo Editor: Meghan Lamb
Cartographer: Roberta Stockwell
Indexer: Cheryl Lenser

Front cover photos, left to right: Left: Big Ben. © Luciano Mortula - LGM / Shutterstock. Middle: Horseguards Parade. © visitlondon.com / Jon Reid. Right: St. Paul's. © iLongLoveKing / Shutterstock.

Back cover photo: Shaftebury Avenue. © peresanz / Shutterstock.

For information on our other products and services, please go to Frommers.com.

Frommer's also publishes its books in a variety of electronic formats. Some content that appears in print may not be available in electronic formats.

Manufactured in China

5 4 3 2 1

About This Guide

Organizing your time. That's what this guide is all about.

Other guides give you long lists of things to see and do and then expect you to fit the pieces together. The Day by Day guides are different. These guides tell you the best of everything, and then they show you how to see it *in the smartest, most time-efficient way.* Our authors have designed detailed itineraries organized by time, neighborhood, or special interest. And each tour comes with a bulleted map that takes you from stop to stop.

Hoping to see where the King lives, or the global treasures of the British Museum? Planning a walk through swanky Chelsea, the "New London" of the East End, or the shopping streets of the West End? Whatever your interest or schedule, the Day by Days give you the smartest routes to follow. Not only do we take you to the top attractions, hotels, and restaurants, but we also help you access those special moments that locals get to experience—those "finds" that turn tourists into travelers.

The Day by Days are also your top choice if you're looking for one complete guide for all your travel needs. The best hotels and restaurants for every budget, the greatest shopping values, the wildest nightlife—it's all here.

Why should you trust our judgment? Because our authors personally visit each place they write about. They're an independent lot who say what they think and would never include places they wouldn't recommend to their best friends. They're also open to suggestions from readers. If you'd like to contact them, please send your comments our way at feedback@frommers.com, and we'll pass them on.

Enjoy your Day by Day guide—the most helpful travel companion you can buy. And have the trip of a lifetime.

About the Author

Donald Strachan is a writer and journalist whose work has been published worldwide, including in the *UK Telegraph* and *Guardian, National Geographic Traveller* magazine, and CNN.com. Over the years, he has written about everything London-related, from craft beer and coffee to shopping and spooky walks. He has authored or coauthored several guidebooks for Frommer's, including *Frommer's England & Scotland* and multiple editions of *Frommer's Italy.*

An Additional Note

Please be advised that travel information is subject to change at any time—and this is especially true of prices. We therefore suggest that you write or call ahead for confirmation when making your travel plans. The authors, editors, and publisher cannot be held responsible for the experiences of readers while traveling. Your safety is important to us, however, so we encourage you to stay alert and be aware of your surroundings.

Star Ratings, Icons & Abbreviations

Every hotel, restaurant, and attraction listing in this guide has been ranked for quality, value, service, amenities, and special features using a star-rating system. Hotels, restaurants, attractions, shopping, and nightlife are rated on a scale of zero stars (recommended) to three stars (exceptional). In addition to the star-rating system, we also use a **kids** icon to point out the best bets for families. Within each tour, we recommend cafes, bars, or restaurants where you can take a break. Each of these stops appears in a shaded box marked with a coffee-cup-shaped bullet 🍵.

Frommers.com

Now that you have this guidebook to help you plan a great trip, visit our website at **www.frommers.com** for additional travel information on more than 4,000 destinations. We update features regularly to give you instant access to the most current trip-planning information available. At Frommers.com, you'll find scoops on the best airfares, lodging rates, and car rental bargains. You can even book your travel online through our reliable travel booking partners. Other popular features include:

- Online updates of our most popular guidebooks
- Vacation sweepstakes and contest giveaways
- Newsletters highlighting the hottest travel trends
- Award-winning weekly podcasts interviewing some of the top names in travel

An Invitation to the Reader

In researching this book, we discovered many wonderful places—hotels, restaurants, shops, and more. We're sure you'll find others. Please tell us about them, so we can share the information with your fellow travelers in upcoming editions. If you were disappointed with a recommendation, we'd love to know that, too. Please write to: Support@FrommerMedia.com.

16 Favorite
Moments

16 Favorite Moments

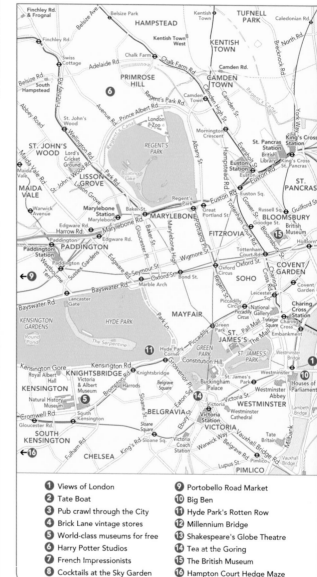

1. Views of London
2. Tate Boat
3. Pub crawl through the City
4. Brick Lane vintage stores
5. World-class museums for free
6. Harry Potter Studios
7. French Impressionists
8. Cocktails at the Sky Garden
9. Portobello Road Market
10. Big Ben
11. Hyde Park's Rotten Row
12. Millennium Bridge
13. Shakespeare's Globe Theatre
14. Tea at the Goring
15. The British Museum
16. Hampton Court Hedge Maze

Previous page: Riders enjoying views of the London cityscape from the London Eye Ferris wheel.

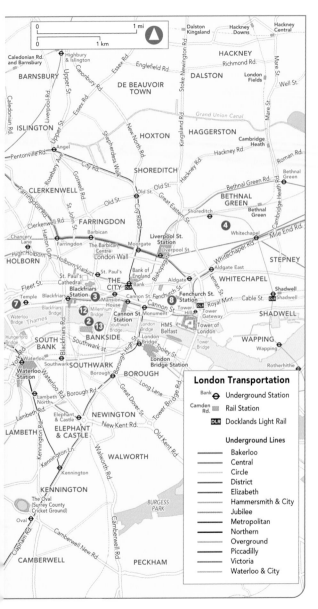

London Transportation

Bank ⊖	Underground Station
Camden Rd. ▨	Rail Station
DLR	Docklands Light Rail

Underground Lines

——— Bakerloo
——— Central
——— Circle
——— District
——— Elizabeth
——— Hammersmith & City
——— Jubilee
——— Metropolitan
——— Northern
——— Overground
——— Piccadilly
——— Victoria
——— Waterloo & City

You can explore the wonders of science, history, art, and nature at world-class museums, eat yourself to a bigger dress size at top-notch restaurants, marvel at just how much gold and jewelry fill the palaces and castles, and say you've "done" London. But to get to *know* London, you need to experience the special moments that reveal the city's true character. Below are some of the best.

A pub-crawl stop at the Coach & Horses in Covent Garden.

❶ Find hidden panoramas that won't cost you a dime. By all means ride the London Eye wheel for the picture-perfect shot of London's far-reaching cityscape. It's great, especially on a "night flight" when lights come on across the city. But London has plenty more to reveal to those who know where to look, from a rooftop garden surrounded by skyscrapers, a park in Royal Greenwich, or the vantage point from which the Gunpowder Plotters hoped to see Parliament burn. And yes, you read right: They're all 100% free to reach. *See p 13,* ❾ *; p 63,* ❽ *; p 74,* ❾*.*

❷ Have an art-to-art aboard the Tate Boat. Running between the sister museums of Tate Britain and Tate Modern, the Thames Clipper boat allows you to instantly swap an eyeful of paintings and installations for views of iconic Thames sights, as it speeds past Parliament and Big Ben. *See p 17.*

❸ Get to know Londoners in their natural habitat, with a pub crawl in the City. A trip to a traditional boozer can combine many interests, such as history (many pubs have been pulling pints for a *very* long time), dining, pub games, and of course, a wide range of drinks to sample. Be sure to pace yourself or stick to now-common (and much improved) zero-beers, which are attracting sober Londoners back to this British institution. *See p 138.*

❹ Shop for vintage styles around Brick Lane, home to London's most fashion-forward thrift stores. Come on a weekend and this corner of the East End is even more alive with street markets and endless street food. *See p 90.*

❺ Enjoy the finest free museum collections on the planet. And second place isn't even close. Entire buildings dedicated to painting, sculpture, history, finance, disease, decorative arts, and a whole lot

Egyptian cat at the British Museum.

more would cost you hundreds of dollars anywhere else but London.

6 Taste what a real wizard can do with fire, when you dine with a new generation of pyro-inspired London chefs. You don't need to spend big to enjoy huge seasonal British, Basque, and Sri Lankan flavors cooked in the oldest way of all, over a roaring flame. *See chapter 6.*

7 Journey to 19th-century Paris, without leaving London. The top floor of the Courtauld Gallery has a truly astonishing collection of French Impressionist works. I could stare back at Manet's Folies-Bergère barmaid for hours. *See p 41, ❹.*

8 Drink cocktails in the Sky Garden, a unique glass-covered space at the top of the "Walkie-Talkie," one of the capital's newest skyscrapers. The bar provides the best opportunity to drink in London from above, with even newer towers sprouting up on all sides. *See p 131.*

9 Haggle for a bargain at Portobello Road Market, either at the open-air stalls or in its warrenlike indoor arcades. You may get 10% to 15% off the asking price, which everyone involved knows is set just for negotiation. Saturday's the big day for this famous antiques market, and part of the fun is sharing

the street with crowds of bargain hunters and loiterers. *See p 96.*

10 Listen to Big Ben strike the hour. The bongs at midnight on December 31 obviously get the biggest cheer, but this is a very London pleasure whatever the hour. It's the bell itself that's named Big Ben, even though most assign that name to the whole clock tower. Although the bell has a crack in it and can't sound an E note, its chimed aria from Handel's *Messiah* is the undisputed aural symbol of London. *See p 10, ❷.*

11 Ride down Hyde Park's Rotten Row on horseback and you'll feel like a character in an 18th-century English novel—at least, if you ignore the passing joggers, skaters, and cyclists. There's no better way to absorb the atmosphere of London's most popular park. Only skilled riders should let their horses try a canter; novices will still enjoy the experience at walking speed. *See p 100, ❼.*

12 Stand above the midpoint of the Thames on the Millennium Bridge, which spans not just the river but also the centuries, with St. Paul's Cathedral on one side and Tate Modern on the other. Views of the cityscape are even more impressive at sunrise and sunset. *See p 11, ❼.*

Portobello Road Market in Notting Hill.

Soldiers on horseback in Hyde Park.

13 Become part of the play at Shakespeare's Globe Theatre as one of the "groundlings" who stand in front of the stage, much as the rabble did during Shakespeare's time. You never know when the actors might mingle among you to bellow out their lines. It's a truly Elizabethan experience, minus the pickpockets and the spitting. *See p 150.*

14 Stuff yourself with a full afternoon tea at the Goring. This deluxe hotel rises to the task, impressing everyone with an army of sandwiches, scones with clotted cream, and cakes—all washed down with tea from their vast menu. Don't make dinner plans: You won't be hungry. *See p 116.*

15 Explore the reach of Empire at the British Museum, where priceless treasures acquired from all parts of the globe—including the Rosetta Stone and the Parthenon Marbles—testify to the power that Britain once exerted over the farthest reaches of the world. And give an insight into just how greedy its adventurers were. *See p 28.*

16 Lose your way inside Hampton Court Palace's Hedge Maze, with winding paths that cover nearly half a mile. When you extricate yourself from its clutches, stroll through centuries of architectural styles featured at this stunning palace, the country home of many an English monarch, including Henry VIII. *See p 50,* **10.** ●

The Hampton Court Hedge Maze.

1 The Best Full-Day Tours

The Best **in One Day**

London Transportation

Bank ⊖	Underground Station
Camden Rd. ▦	Rail Station
DLR	Docklands Light Rail

Underground Lines

———— Bakerloo
———— Central
———— Circle
———— District
———— Elizabeth
———— Hammersmith & City
———— Jubilee
———— Metropolitan
———— Northern
———— Overground
———— Piccadilly
———— Victoria
———— Waterloo & City

① Westminster Abbey
② Big Ben
③ Houses of Parliament
④ Churchill War Rooms
⑤ Swan at the Globe
⑥ Shakespeare's Globe Theatre
⑦ Millennium Bridge
⑧ St. Paul's Cathedral
⑨ London Eye

Previous page: Buckingham Palace, as seen from the Mall.

This packed tour encapsulates "Iconic London" in all its postcard-friendly glory. You'll be visiting attractions, including Westminster Abbey and St. Paul's, that have been familiar to travelers for centuries, as well as more recent arrivals, such as the London Eye, and modern re-creations of the past, such as Shakespeare's Globe. Total time: 1 very busy day. Total history covered: More than 1,000 years. Chance you'll spot a red telephone box: 100%. START: **Tube to Westminster.**

Look up! Westminster Abbey's ceiling is exquisite.

❶ ★★★ Westminster Abbey. Images from this 1,000-year-old abbey were beamed across the globe during the 2023 coronation of King Charles III. It is one of the finest examples of medieval architecture in Europe and a giant shrine to the nation, housing some 3,300 memorials to monarchs, nobles, and other great British figures from down the ages. Edward III, Mary Queen of Scots, Elizabeth I (whose death mask was the model for her tomb's figure), and Henry V, the hero of Agincourt, all have elaborately decorated sarcophagi. Purcell and Elgar, Newton, and Darwin are also buried here. Don't miss the Gothic fan vault of the **Henry VIII Lady Chapel** (reflected in a large mirror for close-up viewing) and its elaborately carved choir stalls; England's oldest surviving door, from 1050, beside the **Chapter House;** and the treasure-filled **Queen's Diamond Jubilee Galleries.** At **Poets' Corner** are monuments and tombs of literary such names as Chaucer, Shakespeare, Austen, Henry James, and Dickens. ⏱ *1 ½ hr. Dean's Yard.* ☎ *020/7222-5152. westminster-abbey.org. £27 adults, £24 seniors & students, £12 children 6–17 (1 child enters free with full-price adult ticket); half-price "Lates" admission Wed after 4:30pm.*

Houses of Parliament at dusk.

Mon–Fri 9:30am–4:30pm, Wed until 7pm, Sat 9:30am–4pm. Last admission 1 hr. before closing; reserve timed admission slot online to avoid long lines. Tube: Westminster.

❷ ★★ **Big Ben.** In 2012, the iconic clock tower of the Palace of Westminster was officially named the Elizabeth Tower to mark the monarch's then-60 years on the throne. Most, however, continue to call it by its nickname, Big Ben, even though this technically refers only to the tower's largest bell. This 14-tonne (15-ton) bell, installed in 1858, is believed to have been named after the portly commissioner of public works at the time, Sir Benjamin Hall. A long-running refurbishment was completed in 2023, and visitors can once again ascend the tower's 334 spiral steps by 90-minute guided tour to stand next to the bell when it chimes. Alas, this busy itinerary only allows time to grab a snapshot from ground level. If you have a fervent interest, bookmark the tour for another day. *Near St. Stephen's*

Entrance of Westminster Palace. parliament.uk/visiting. Tours usually go on sale 2nd Wed of month; £25 adults, £10 children 11–17 (prebooking essential). Tube: Westminster.

❸ ★★ **Houses of Parliament.** The immense 3-hectare (7.4-acre) Palace of Westminster, a splendid example of Gothic Revival architecture by Charles Barry, dates to 1840; the original palace was all but destroyed by fire in 1834. It's home to some 650 M.P.s (Members of Parliament, the elected representatives of the people) of the House of Commons and the 770-plus appointed members of the House of Lords, who scrutinize decisions made in the Commons. You may observe debates for free from the public galleries in both houses, but long lines for the big debates (such as Prime Minister's Questions, Wed at noon) usually make this attraction better for a quick photo opportunity than a lengthy visit. The main exceptions are on Saturdays throughout the year and Tuesday through Friday during

Parliament's many recess periods, when Parliament is open for guided and self-guided tours that visit both chambers of the legislature. *Old Palace Yard. parliament.uk/visiting. Free admission to debates: See schedule at whatson.parliament.uk. Guided tours (1½ hr.): £32 adults, £26 ages 16–24, £11 children 5–15 (self-guided multimedia tours slightly cheaper); check website for tour times and to book tickets. Tube: Westminster.*

④ ★★★ kids Churchill War Rooms. Tour the underground headquarters from where Britain's WWII prime minister directed the war against Hitler, including a secret Telephone Room with a direct line to the U.S. president. After your visit, jump on the Tube's Jubilee Line at Westminster Station and ride two stops to Southwark. ① *1 hr. See p 81,* **②**.

The **⑤ ★ Swan at the Globe** is a fine choice for a restorative break and has a Thames-side view of London. The menu in the bar features reasonably priced English favorites, such as shepherd's pie or fish and chips, salads, and British cheese-sharing platters, while the restaurant is a fancier (and more expensive) affair. *21 Globe Walk (off Thames Path).* ☎ *020/7928-9444. swanlondon.co.uk. £–££.*

⑥ ★★ Shakespeare's Globe Theatre. Even if you don't have tickets to watch a play (p 150), the Globe is still a fascinating place to visit. It was rebuilt in painstaking detail on what was a parking lot near the site of the original theater. Only tools authentic to the period of the original were used in its construction: Icosagonal (20-sided) in shape, it has central London's only

thatched roof because thatching was banned after the Great Fire of 1666. In the late 1500s/early 1600s, Shakespeare's works were performed to delight the nobility (who sat in the tiers) as well as the rabble (who stood in front of the stage). You can choose either option when purchasing tickets, weighing comfort versus proximity to the action. Changing displays at the onsite exhibition focus on such topics as Elizabethan stagecraft, the frost fairs of medieval London (when the Thames would freeze solid and people partied on the river for days), or the juicy history of nearby Southwark, once a haven of prostitutes and thieves. ① *1½ hr. 21 New Globe Walk.* ☎ *020/7401-9919. shakespearesglobe.com. Admission to Globe Story & Tour: £25 adults, £18 children 5–15. Daily 9:30am–5pm (prebooking recommended; no tours during afternoon theater matinees). Tube: London Bridge or Southwark.*

⑦ ★ kids Millennium Bridge. This silver sliver of a footbridge

Millennium Bridge.

A service at St. Paul's Cathedral, viewed from the Whispering Gallery.

connecting Bankside to the City is a wonderful spot from which to take photos of the surrounding landmarks (and note the incongruity of the Globe nestled among its 20th-c. neighbors). When it first opened in 2000, it swayed and was temporarily shut down to be stabilized—and Londoners still refer to it as the "wobbly bridge." ◷ *10 min. Tube: Southwark or Blackfriars.*

⑧ ★★★ kids St. Paul's Cathedral. The dome of St. Paul's has been the defining silhouette of the London skyline since its construction after the Great Fire of 1666. It may not be the city's tallest structure anymore, but no modern skyscraper (even the much-admired "Gherkin") is held in such affection—or inspires the same awe—as Sir Christopher Wren's masterpiece. The cathedral was the culmination of Wren's unique and much-acclaimed fusion of classical (the exterior Greek-style columns)

and baroque (the ornate interior decorations) architecture. The **Whispering Gallery** (alas, sometimes closed) is a miracle of engineering, in which you can hear the murmurs of another person from across a large gallery. The 528 stairs to the **Golden Gallery** are demanding, but you're rewarded with a magnificent view not only of London but also of the interior of the cathedral 85m (279 ft.) below. Wren—who is buried in the cathedral's **Crypt** alongside Admiral Lord Nelson, Wellington, and other military notables—considered it his ultimate achievement. Free audio guides are included in the admission price. Christian services are held daily and free to attend for worship. ◷ *1½ hr. Ludgate Hill.* ☎ *020/7246-8357. stpauls.co.uk. £20.50 adults, £18.50 seniors & students, £9 children 6–17, £50 family (2+3). Mon–Sat 8:30am–4pm. Tube: St. Paul's.*

❾ ★★ kids London Eye. The huge Ferris wheel that solemnly rotates one revolution per half-hour is already an icon of the city and now begrudgingly accepted by even the most hardened traditionalist. Buying a timed ticket well in advance is pretty much essential (thus securing the prices listed below), but your ride may be tinged with disappointment if you get a gray day. Instead, a later "night flight" guarantees twinkling lights to end your busy day. Same-day tickets are sometimes available in the off season. Don't forget your camera. ⏰ *1 hr. South Bank (at Westminster Bridge). londoneye.com. £31 adults, £27.50 children 3–15, £28 per person family ticket. Sept–June daily 11am–6pm, July–Aug 10am–8:30pm. Closed 3 weeks in Jan. Tube: Westminster or Waterloo.*

The London Eye.

The Best **in Two Days**

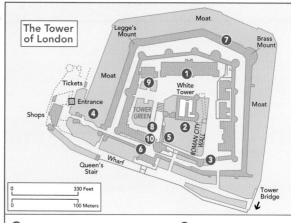

The Tower
of London

1 Crown Jewels Entrance
2 White Tower
3 Battlements
4 Yeoman Warders
5 The Ravens
6 Medieval Palace
7 Royal Beasts
8 Torture at the Tower
9 Imprisonment at theTower
10 Bloody Tower

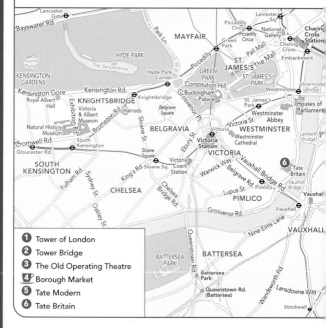

1 Tower of London
2 Tower Bridge
3 The Old Operating Theatre
4 Borough Market
5 Tate Modern
6 Tate Britain

London Transportation

Bank ⊖	Underground Station
Camden Rd. 🔲	Rail Station
DLR	Docklands Light Rail

Underground Lines

———— Bakerloo
———— Central
———— Circle
———— District
———— Elizabeth
———— Hammersmith & City
———— Jubilee
———— Metropolitan
———— Northern
———— Overground
———— Piccadilly
———— Victoria
———— Waterloo & City

On a second day, you'll delve deeper into the capital's history, exploring the buildings, jewels, and ghosts that populate the Tower of London; British art at Tate Britain; and the gruesome horrors of our medical past at the Old Operating Theatre. You'll also experience the Tate Modern and traverse the Thames by boat, now (as always) the watery soul of the city. START: **Tube to Tower Hill.**

Beefeater at the Tower of London.

1 ★★★ kids Tower of London. Commissioned by William the Conqueror in 1078, this fortress was added to by subsequent generations of kings and queens and reflects the range of England's architectural styles over a millennium. The Tower has a bloody past marked by power struggles, executions, and cruelty: The young nephews of Richard III were murdered here (probably) in 1483; two of Henry VIII's six wives (Anne Boleyn and Catherine Howard) were beheaded on Tower Green, as was England's 9-day queen, Lady Jane Grey. Yeoman Warders (or "Beefeaters") give gore-filled talks all day long, and actors offer living-history lessons as they wander about in period costume. The **Crown Jewels** (centerpiece of a new exhibit inaugurated in 2023) are the most popular sight, just edging out the **Torture at the Tower** exhibit; the two together represent the awful accouterments of power

Tower Ghosts

The Tower of London, said to be the most haunted spot in England, overflows with supernatural manifestations of tormented souls.

The ghost of Queen Anne Boleyn (executed in 1536 on a trumped-up charge of treason after she failed to produce a male heir for Henry VIII) is most frequently spotted. The tragic shades of the Little Princes—allegedly murdered by Richard III in 1483—have been spied in the Bloody Tower. Ghostly reenactments of the Tower Green beheading of the Countess of Salisbury—who was slowly hacked to death by her inept executioner on May 27, 1541—have been seen on its anniversary. The screams of Guy Fawkes, who gave up his co-conspirators in the Gunpowder Plot under torture, reputedly still echo around the grounds.

Other spirits you may encounter (the no-nonsense Tower guards have had run-ins with them all) include Sir Walter Raleigh, Lady Jane Grey, and Henry VI.

Sail the Tate Boat

The Tate Boat ferry service between the two Tate galleries on opposite banks of the Thames is one of London's more useful tourist creations. The same people who built the London Eye designed the ferry's dramatic Millbank Pier. One of the colorful catamaran was decorated by a former *enfant terrible* of the British contemporary art scene, Damian Hirst. The 20-minute service—formally denoted as lines RB1 and RB2—stops off at the London Eye en route (p 13, **⑨**) and makes a convenient and scenic way to get from one to the other.

Alas, it's not free. One-way tickets cost £9.50 adults, £4.75 kids 5 to 15, free for kids 4 and under. If you have a London Travelcard (p 173), you get a good discount. Tickets can be bought online, at the pier, or via the Uber app, or simply tap your Oyster Card on the reader (p 173). The Tate Boat runs daily every 20 to 30 minutes between 9am and 4:15pm (later on weekends). For service times, check tate.org.uk/visit/tate-boat.

(and have the longest lines). The haunted—and haunting—Tower will thrill students of history and entertain kids too. ⏱ *2 hr. Tower Hill.* ☎ *0333/320-6000. hrp.org.uk/ TowerOfLondon. £33 adults, £27 seniors, £17 children 5–15, £52–£82 family. Tues–Sat 9am–5:30pm; Sun–Mon 10am–5:30pm; closes 4:30pm Nov–Feb. Tube: Tower Hill.*

② ★ **kids Tower Bridge.** This picture-perfect bascule bridge—a term derived from the French for "seesaw"—has spanned the Thames since 1894. There's no denying the physical beauty of the neo-Gothic

Tower Bridge.

structure: Its skeleton of steel girders is clothed in ornate masonry using Cornish granite and Portland stone designed to harmonize elegantly with the Tower. Its lower span opens and closes regularly thanks to some heavy-duty hydraulics (a board next to the bridge tells you when, or check towerbridge.org.uk/lift-times). Find out more at the **Tower Bridge Exhibition,** where you can also ascend to the bridge's top-level walkways for a bird's-eye view of the Tower of London and the Thames, 43m (141 ft.) below through a glass floor. (Acrophobics may prefer to skip that bit.) ⏱ *1 hr. Tower Bridge Rd.* ☎ *020/7403-3761. towerbridge. org.uk. £12.30 adults, £9 seniors, £6 children 5–15, £22–£37 family. Daily 9:30am–5:30pm. Tube: Tower Hill.*

③ ★★ **kids The Old Operating Theatre & Herb Garret.** A wooden table where operations—usually amputations—were performed without anesthetic or antiseptic (leather restraints held the patient in place, while the only pain relief was provided by alcohol

An Alternate Day-Trip for Pottering

Visitors may prefer to make a pilgrimage from central London to explore the universe of the world's most famous wizard (sorry, Gandalf). At **Warner Bros. The Making of Harry Potter** (☎ 0800/640-4550; wbstudiotour.co.uk), vast studios house the genuine sets where all eight of the original movies were filmed. After a half-hour talk and tour of the **Great Hall,** you're free to explore at your pace, which takes at least 2 hours. You'll walk along **Diagon Alley,** visit **Gringotts,** board the **Hogwarts Express,** and see thousands of the props, costumes, and animatronic creatures that every fan knows. There's enough insight into the craft of moviemaking to fill Hermione's bottomless bag. Booking a timeslot in advance is essential: The first tour of the day is generally 8:30am, with the final one between 4pm and 6:30pm, depending on the season. Admission costs £51.50 adults, £40 children 5–15, £160 family ticket: Steep, but well worth it for fans. To get to the Studios, take the train to Watford Junction and then board a free shuttle bus.

and the surgeon's speed); an early pair of forceps; and other instruments of outdated medical practices will fast cure any grumbles you may have about modern hospitals. ⏱ 40 min. 9a St. Thomas's St. ☎ 020/7188-2679. oldoperating theatre.com. £7.50 adults, £6 seniors & students, £4.50 children 17 & under, £18 family. Thurs–Sun 10:30am–5pm. Tube: London Bridge.

Borough Market.

An almost limitless menu awaits at ④ ★★★ **Borough Market,** where produce and street food inspired by every corner of the globe is hawked. A personal favorite? A hunk of Montgomery's Cheddar from Neal's Yard Dairy (p 93), paired with a crunchy Braeburn apple from a market stall. Whatever you choose, grab and go: Borough offers a joyous bounty but is insanely busy on weekends and most of the summer. You'll find a quieter spot by the riverbank. *Stoney St. £.*

⑤ ★★★ **kids Tate Modern.** The world's most popular modern art museum is housed in the gargantuan shell of a converted 1950s brick power station and its modern extension, the **Blavatnik Building,** which resembles a twisted, truncated, brick pyramid. Through the main entrance, you enter a vast space, the **Turbine Hall,** where temporary exhibitions are held—the bigger and more ambitious, the better. Highlights have included 100 million ceramic sunflower seeds covering the floor (Ai

Dumbledore's Office at Warner Bros. The Making of Harry Potter.

Weiwei) and a maze made from 14,000 polyethylene boxes (Rachel Whiteread). Spread over multiple levels, the permanent collection encompasses a great body of art dating from 1900 to right now. It includes such heavy hitters as Matisse, Lichtenstein, Picasso, Dalí, Duchamp, and Beuys and is arranged according to movement—Surrealism, for example—single artists (such as Bridget Riley), geography (perspectives from São Paolo or Tokyo), or curated themes, such as Art after Catastrophe. The large complex has multiple cafes and bars, plus one of London's best art bookshops. The layout can be a little bewildering: Download a free floor plan from the website before your visit. ○ *1½ hr. Bankside.* ☎ *020/7887-8888. tate.org. uk. Free admission, except for some temporary exhibitions. Daily 10am–6pm. Tube: Southwark or Blackfriars.*

❻ ★★ Tate Britain. Housed in a charming neoclassical building, which looks a bit like a miniature British Museum, Tate Britain opened in 1897 thanks to donations of money and art from sugar mogul Sir Henry Tate. Fresh from a 2023 re-hang that places very different works and periods "in conversation" with each other, the country's finest collection of British art covers the period from the 16th century to the present day. Highlights include an unparalleled collection of art by revolutionary landscape painter J. M. W. Turner (1775–1851), who bequeathed most of his works to the museum. Other notable artists whose work adorns the walls include satirist William Hogarth, polymath William Blake, members of the 19th-century Pre-Raphaelite Brotherhood, and late-20th-century British artists, such as Barbara Hepworth and Tracy Emin. ○ *1½ hr. Millbank.* ☎ *020/7887-8888. tate. org.uk. Free admission, except for temporary exhibitions. Daily 10am–6pm. Tube: Pimlico.*

A poster exhibit at the Tate Modern.

The Best **in Three Days**

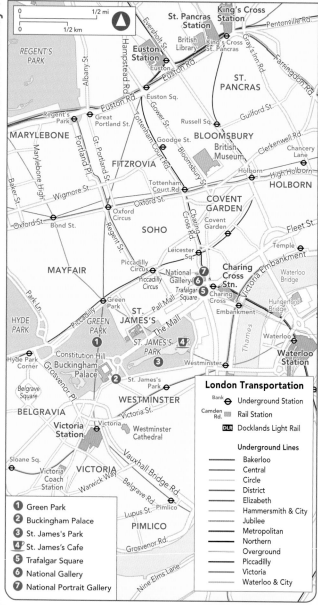

| | 0 | 1/2 mi |
| 0 | 1/2 km | |

London Transportation

Bank ⊖	Underground Station
Camden Rd. ▪	Rail Station
DLR	Docklands Light Rail

Underground Lines

———	Bakerloo
———	Central
———	Circle
———	District
———	Elizabeth
———	Hammersmith & City
———	Jubilee
———	Metropolitan
———	Northern
———	Overground
———	Piccadilly
———	Victoria
———	Waterloo & City

1 Green Park
2 Buckingham Palace
3 St. James's Park
4 St. James's Cafe
5 Trafalgar Square
6 National Gallery
7 National Portrait Gallery

Setting a gentler pace than your first 2 days, this tour begins with some of London's quintessential British attractions—sweeping royal parks and the pomp and ceremony of the Changing of the Guard—and finishes at the National Gallery and National Portrait Gallery, the nation's art collection, which celebrated its 200th birthday in 2024. START: Tube to Green Park.

1 ★ kids Green Park. London's royal parks are often busy affairs, filled with flowerbeds, statues, ponds, playgrounds, and more, but all you'll find here are acres of rolling green lawns and tall, shady trees. In summer, scores of local workers sun their lunch hours away either on the grass or on the stripy deckchairs (£3/hr.) that represent the park's one formal facility. Founded in 1660 to allow Charles II to travel between St. James's Park and Hyde Park without leaving royal soil, the park's stripped-back nature supposedly dates from the time the queen caught Charles giving flowers from the park to another woman. In a rage, she had all the flowerbeds torn up. ⏱ 15 min. royalparks.org.uk. Tube: Green Park.

2 ★ Buckingham Palace. "Buck House," the royals' famous abode in London (if the yellow-and-red Royal standard is flying, it means the monarch is home), is the setting for the pageantry of **Changing the Guard,** a London tradition that attracts more people than it warrants. A better place to see all the queen's horses and all the queen's men in action is at Horse Guards Parade (p 82, **7**). But if you're determined to watch the guards change here, arrive a half-hour early to get a spot by the statue of Victoria; it offers a reasonably good view. The ceremony begins at 11am sharp every Monday, Wednesday, Friday, and Sunday all summer—in theory, anyway; it's often canceled in bad weather. ⏱ 45 min. See p 37, **2**.

3 ★★ kids St. James's Park. Southeast of Green Park, this is arguably central London's prettiest park. It's difficult to believe that this was, up until the 18th century, the center of a notorious scene, where prostitutes conducted their business and drunken rakes took unsteady aim at dueling opponents. It's now very respectable, with a wildfowl pond and weeping willows. ⏱ 30 min. royalparks.org.uk.

In the northeast sector of the park, **4 kids St. James's Café** is a bright, modern spot with picturesque views from its roof terrace. In St. James's Park. ☎ 020/7839-1149. £.

5 kids Trafalgar Square. Where a visit to this square once involved battling traffic and dodging pigeons, a part-pedestrianization and a ban on bird-feeding means it

A riot of tulips at Buckingham Palace.

The National Gallery in Trafalgar Square.

is now once again possible to appreciate the grand surroundings. Bordering the square are the **National Gallery** (see below) on the northern side; **St. Martin-in-the-Fields Church** to the east; and in the northwest corner, the **"Fourth Plinth,"** which supports (literally) temporary art installations. Towering above everything is **Nelson's Column,** a pillar topped with a statue of Britain's most revered naval commander, Horatio, Viscount Nelson. The square is named for his most famous and (for him) fatal victory, the 1805 Battle of Trafalgar. This is often the focal point of rallies, demonstrations, and national celebrations. ⏱ *15 min.*

⑥ ★★★ kids National Gallery. Leave most of the afternoon for two world-class museums that sit roughly where the stables of King Henry VIII used to be. Founded with a collection of 38 paintings bought by the government, the National celebrated its 200th birthday in 2024. It is home to some 2,300 works charting the development of western European painting from 1250 to the early 1900s. *Note:* A 2025 rebuild of the Sainsbury Wing entrance may cause reshuffling of major works' locations.

Faces from yesterday and today at the National Portrait Gallery.

National Gallery Highlights

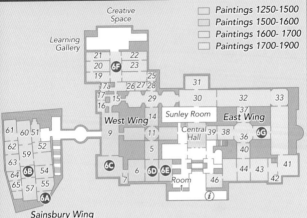

Paintings 1250-1500
Paintings 1500-1600
Paintings 1600-1700
Paintings 1700-1900

Start in the **6A** ★★★ **Sainsbury Wing's Room 56,** where you'll find early European works, including Van Eyck's haunting *Arnolfini Portrait.* Note the words inscribed over the mirror: JAN VAN EYCK WAS HERE/1434. For a contrast in mood, go to **6B** **Room 58** for Botticelli's voluptuous *Venus and Mars.* The **6C** **West Wing's Room 8** has an ethereal Raphael painting known as *The Madonna of the Pinks* (1506) as well as a couple of Michelangelos. Holbein's *Ambassadors* is in **6D** **Room 4;** the skull in the foreground looks distorted unless you look at it from the right-hand side. Pay your respects to Titian in **6E** **Room 2,** and then leave the Renaissance for the **6F** **North Wing** and Dutch, French, and Spanish masterpieces from 1600 to 1800, including Rembrandt's self-portrait in Room 22 and Velazquez's controversial *Rokeby Venus* (Room 30). Finish at the **6G** **East Wing** and the works of Impressionists van Gogh (including his *Sunflowers* in Room 43), Monet, and Renoir. ⏱ 2½ hr. Trafalgar Sq. ☎ 020/7747-2885. nationalgallery. org.uk. Free admission, except temporary exhibitions. Daily 10am–6pm, till 9pm Fri. Tube: Charing Cross.

7 ★★ **National Portrait Gallery.** The NPG is the place to put faces to the names of those who shaped Britain politically, socially, and culturally. It reopened in 2023 after a renovation and re-hang intended to reflect modern Britain. Start at the top with the perennially popular Tudors, the royal dynasty that ruled for almost 150 years from 1485—a moment that coincided with the birth of portraiture in England. The new **History Makers Now** gallery captures modern Britain from poet Kae Tempest to Oscar-winning director Steve McQueen. ⏱ 1¼ hr. St. Martin's Place. ☎ 020/7306-0055. npg.org. uk. Free admission, except temporary exhibitions. Sun–Thurs 10:30am–6pm, Fri & Sat 10:30am–9pm. Tube: Leicester Sq.

The Best in Four Days

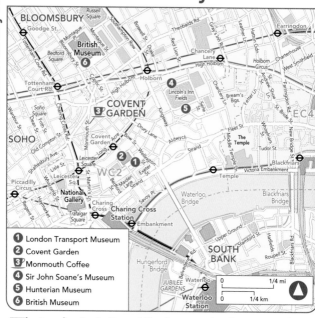

1 London Transport Museum
2 Covent Garden
3 Monmouth Coffee
4 Sir John Soane's Museum
5 Hunterian Museum
6 British Museum

The tour begins in Covent Garden, once London's general store and now ringed by quality shopping and dining chains, pop-ups, and quirky street performers. Continue to the gloriously elegant clutter at the Sir John Soane's Museum, which serves as the perfect appetizer for perhaps the finest museum of human civilization anywhere, the British Museum. START: **Tube to Covent Garden.**

1 ★★ kids **London Transport Museum.** This is a real winner with kids—but not only for them. It's also a fascinating collection that traces the technological and social history of London transport, focusing of course on the world's first subway: the Tube. The museum offers the chance to climb aboard a stagecoach, ride a double-decker Omnibus, and peer inside an old Underground train. Admission tickets permit unlimited entry for a year. For a deeper look into urban

transport, the museum's super **Hidden London** tours take you to subterranean tramways and abandoned metro stations—but you'll need to book ahead online. ⏱ 1½ hr. The Piazza. ☎ 0343/222-5000. ltmuseum.co.uk. £24 adults, free for children 17 & under. Daily 10am–6pm. Tube: Covent Garden.

2 ★ kids **Covent Garden.** The great fruit and vegetable bazaar that was this area's centerpiece moved out in the early 1970s, but glorious 19th-century market

Skylight crammed with art at Sir John Sloane's Museum.

buildings remain. **Jubilee Market** (jubileemarket.co.uk), with crafts and inexpensive souvenirs, is on the southern side of the arcade. A motley collection of jugglers and physical comedians perform on the **Piazza,** while in the main market building you can have a pint, grab a burger, or maybe experience an impromptu performance by professionals from the **Royal Opera House** (p 146), which faces the arcade. Just north, the **Seven Dials** neighborhood—a notorious slum, or "rookery," in the Georgian period—has modish shopping streets. ⏱ *30 min. coventgarden. london. Tube: Covent Garden.*

One of London's oldest artisanal coffee roasters, 3️⃣ ★ **Monmouth Coffee** began life here in the basement of what's now their café. The best spot around Seven Dials for pastries, cakes, and of course a great cup of joe. Closed Sun. *27 Monmouth St. monmouthcoffee. co.uk. £.*

4️⃣ ★★★ **Sir John Soane's Museum.** The distinguished architect Sir John Soane (1753–1837) took hoarding to a whole new level. The bulk of his collection was amassed at the height of empire, when antiquities could be removed from their country of origin and displayed casually in one's home—so long as you were English, naturally. Ancient tablets, sculptures, paintings (including William Hogarth's satirical parable-in-paint, *A Rake's Progress,* and works by Turner and Canaletto), architectural models, loot from Hadrian's Villa near Rome, and even the Egyptian sarcophagus of Seti I are strewn around in no particular order: This is essentially how he left it to the nation, to be free-to-view forever so long as nothing were moved around (it was, anyway). Haphazardness is part of the unique charm. Free curator-led tours of Soane's apartment and drawing office run once or twice a week. You cannot prebook; just turn up and keep your fingers crossed—the popularity-to-size ratio here is

A collection of heads at the Hunterian Museum.

sky-high, and justly so. 🕐 *1 hr. 12–13 Lincoln's Inn Fields.* ☎ *020/7405-2107. soane.org. Free admission. Wed–Sun 10am–5pm. Tube: Holborn or Chancery Lane.*

❺ ★★ Hunterian Museum. Another 2023 reopening, this offbeat museum directly across the park occupies one wing in the grandiose HQ of the U.K.'s Royal College of Surgeons. Now reorganized to tell the story of surgery from its earliest beginnings (*shudder*) to today, it builds on the collection of esteemed 18th-century surgeon, anatomist, and medical pioneer, John Hunter. Celebrated in his day, his restless inquisitiveness contributed hugely to reducing human suffering—even if many of his methods, including paying grave robbers, would not meet current ethical standards. If you're OK with some potentially upsetting specimens—human fetuses, tumors, cross-sections of elephantiasis, and a stomach wracked by arsenic poisoning, to name a few—it's an extraordinary place. 🕐 *45 min. 38–43 Lincoln's Inn Fields.* ☎ *020/7869-6560. hunterianmuseum.org. Free admission. Tues–Sat 10am–5pm. Tube: Holborn.*

❻ ★★★ kids British Museum. You could spend days exploring this world-renowned museum, but a few hours are enough to get a flavor of what it has to offer—and plan a return visit to cover what you missed. Visit on a Friday and you can stay till 8:30pm to roam, eat, drink, or perhaps attend a talk. 🕐 *3 hr. See tour on p 28.* ●

The British Museum

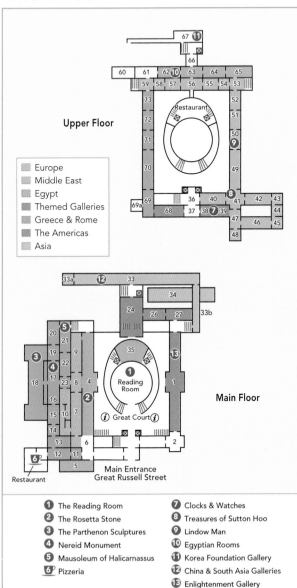

Upper Floor

Restaurant

- ▦ Europe
- ▦ Middle East
- ▦ Egypt
- ▦ Themed Galleries
- ▦ Greece & Rome
- ▦ The Americas
- ▦ Asia

Main Floor

Reading Room

Great Court

Restaurant

Main Entrance
Great Russell Street

- ❶ The Reading Room
- ❷ The Rosetta Stone
- ❸ The Parthenon Sculptures
- ❹ Nereid Monument
- ❺ Mausoleum of Halicarnassus
- ☕ Pizzeria
- ❼ Clocks & Watches
- ❽ Treasures of Sutton Hoo
- ❾ Lindow Man
- ❿ Egyptian Rooms
- ⓫ Korea Foundation Gallery
- ⓬ China & South Asia Galleries
- ⓭ Enlightenment Gallery

Previous page: The Great Hall of the British Museum.

The British Museum, started with a donation by the royal physician and collector Sir Hans Sloane in 1753, opened at a time when the expansion of the British Empire ensured its collection would be as eclectic as it was priceless. Note the frieze above the entrance—it signifies the museum's intention to encompass all the branches of science and the arts. START: **Tube to Holborn, Tottenham Court Road, or Russell Square.**

The Rosetta Stone.

① ★★ The Reading Room.
Located at the center of the **Great Court,** beneath the museum's crazy-paving-style glass roof, this was once the home of the British Library—now moved to more spacious, if less elegant, premises near St. Pancras Station (p 51). It was restored to its 1857 grandeur for the millennium, and today provides a sophisticated setting for temporary exhibitions (entrance fees usually apply). The authors listed on either side of the entrance doors, including Dickens, Marx, Tennyson, Kipling, and Darwin, all once sat within, composing some of history's finest works. ① *15 min.*

② ★★★ The Rosetta Stone.
One of the museum's most prized artifacts is an ancient text engraved on a tablet in three parallel scripts (hieroglyphic, demotic, and Greek) that celebrates the virtues of 13-year-old pharaoh Ptolemy V, who lived in 196 B.C. The tablet was found in 1799 by Napoleon's troops and handed over to the British

Army as part of the Alexandria Treaty of 1802. The text was deciphered in 1822, a breakthrough that allowed scholars to finally decode ancient Middle Eastern hieroglyphics. *Room 4.* ① *10 min.*

③ ★★★ The Parthenon Marbles. The Greek government has been fighting for 2 centuries to get these sculptures—taken from the **Parthenon** by Lord Elgin in 1805—returned to Athens. The B.M. argues that it has provided a safe home for the carvings (including 75m/246 ft. of the original temple frieze), which would otherwise have been chipped away by vandals or degraded by remaining in the open air. The marbles may yet be returned to the Parthenon (which would probably prove a disastrous precedent for the museum, filled as it is with the booty of the world), but don't expect this to happen anytime soon. *Room 18.* ① *20 min.*

④ ★★ Statues of the Nereid Monument. This 4th-century-B.C. Lykian tomb from southwest Turkey arrived at the museum with the Parthenon Marbles in 1816, and its lifelike statuary is almost surreal. Even without their heads, the Nereids (daughters of the sea god Nereus) look as graceful as the ocean waves they personify. *Room 17.* ◔ *10 min.*

⑤ ★★ Mausoleum of Halicarnassus. These are the remains of one of the Seven Wonders of the Ancient World—the breathtaking Ionian Greek tomb built for King Maussollos, from whose name the word "mausoleum" is derived. The huge tomb, some 40m (130 ft.) high, remained undisturbed from 351 B.C. to medieval times, when it was damaged by an earthquake. In 1494, Crusaders used its stones to fortify a castle; in 1846, sections of the tomb's frieze were found at the castle and given to the B.M. Subsequent excavations turned up the remarkably lifelike horse sculpture and a series of lounging figures. *Room 21.* ◔ *15 min.*

Aromas of Italian crispy crusts waft through the galleries of Ancient Mycenae as you approach the **⑥ ★ kids Pizzeria,** a relaxed, cafeteria-style eatery. The made-to-order pizzas are reasonably priced, plus there are main-sized salads and a kids' menu. Open noon till 3pm daily. *Off Room 12. £–££.*

⑦ ★★ Clocks & Watches. The museum's outstanding collection of timepieces dating from the Middle Ages to the present day features the mind-blowing mechanical **Galleon (or "Nef") Clock,** which used to roll along a table announcing dinnertime to guests. Built (in 1585 in Germany) to resemble a medieval ship, the gilt-copper marvel played music, beat drums, and even fired tiny cannons. *Room 39.* ◔ *10 min.*

⑧ ★★★ Treasures of Sutton Hoo. Sutton Hoo was a burial

Historic clock.

ground of the early Anglo-Saxons (including one royal, who literally went down with his 30m [98-ft.] oak ship). When this tomb in Suffolk was excavated in 1939—a tale dramatized in Netflix movie, *The Dig*—previous beliefs about the inferior arts and crafts of England's Dark Ages (around A.D. 625) were confounded, as well-designed musical instruments, glassware, and armor (including the iconic Sutton Hoo helmet, here) were uncovered. *Room 41.* ◔ *20 min.*

⑨ ★★ kids Lindow Man. Don't miss the leathery cadaver of the "Bog Man" (aka "Pete Marsh"), found in 1984 preserved in a peat bog in Cheshire, where he had lain for nearly 2,000 years. The poor man had been struck on the head, garroted, knifed, and then put head-first into the bog. The excessive wounds suggest he died in a sacrificial ritual. *Start of Room 50, on your left.* ◔ *5 min.*

⑩ ★★★ kids Egyptian Rooms. Dedicated to death and the afterlife, rooms 62 and 63 are filled with coffins, sarcophagi, funerary objects, and, of course, mummies. There's even a **mummified cat,** and it's said the ghost of one of the

Practical Matters: The British Museum

The British Museum (☎ 020/7323-8000; britishmuseum.org) main entrance is located on Great Russell Street. Admission is free (£5 donation appreciated), except to temporary exhibitions. The museum is open daily from 10am to 5pm; on Fridays, some galleries remain open until 8:30pm, and free 20-minute Spotlight tours of their key exhibits are offered. Prebooking an entrance time online for these late Friday hours is recommended. Additional touring assistance ranges from a comprehensive, self-directed audio app (£5; Apple/Android) to regular, free 40-minute "Eye-opener" tours that focus on a single theme or gallery; check the website for details or inquire at the Information Desk in the Great Court. A serviceable (and free) museum map points you toward galleries that are often quieter even at the busiest times.

3,000-year-old bandaged corpses still haunts these rooms. ⓒ *20 min.*

⓫ ★★ Korea Foundation Gallery. Even on the busiest day you'll find peace among artefacts from the Korean peninsula since A.D. 300. Alongside ceramics and landscape paintings stands a reconstructed late Joseon *sarangbang* (study) based on designs from Seoul's Changdeokgung Palace. *Room 67.* ⓒ *20 min.*

⓬ ★★★ China & South Asia Galleries. Room 33 is another oasis of calm, housing meditating

Bust of King Ramesses IV.

Buddhas and the Dancing Shiva—a bronze depicting one of India's most famous icons. The intricate frieze of the **Great Amaravati Stupa** (Room 33a), carved in India in the 3rd century B.C., so closely resembles the Parthenon Marbles, you'll wonder about an artistic zeitgeist that seemed to pass unaided across borders and cultures. There are statues of bodhisattvas, Buddhist archetypes, in every medium, from porcelain to metal. ⓒ *25 min.*

⓭ ★ Enlightenment Gallery. "Exploration, Knowledge and Imperialism" is the subtitle of this permanent exhibit—which provides a major clue to its themes. Designed as a library for George III by Sir Robert Smirke, the room is regarded as the finest and largest neoclassical interior hall in London. You'll be reaching for your pince-nez and quill pen as you marvel at the polished mahogany bookshelves stuffed with rare books. Display cases are filled with some 5,000 items that demonstrate the far-reaching, eclectic passions of the 18th-century Enlightenment scholar—the kind of person who helped make the British Museum possible. ⓒ *20 min.*

Victoria & Albert Museum

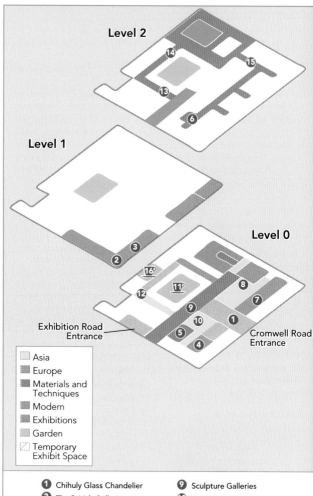

Level 2

Level 1

Level 0

Exhibition Road Entrance

Cromwell Road Entrance

- Asia
- Europe
- Materials and Techniques
- Modern
- Exhibitions
- Garden
- Temporary Exhibit Space

1. Chihuly Glass Chandelier
2. The British Galleries
3. Beasts of Dacre
4. The Raphaels Cartoon
5. Fashion Gallery
6. Ironwork Gallery
7. Medieval & Renaissance Galleries
8. Cast Courts
9. Sculpture Galleries
10. Tippoo's Tiger
11. John Madejski Garden
12. The Ceramic Staircase
13. Gilbert Collection
14. Silver Gallery
15. Gilbert Bayes Sculpture Gallery
16. V&A Café

This museum's 8 miles of galleries are resplendent with the world's greatest and most diverse collection of decorative arts. Opened in 1852 by Prince Albert, this glittering, eclectic treasure trove, known colloquially as the V&A, is made up of millions of pieces of priceless arts and crafts. START: **Tube to South Kensington.**

❶ ★★★ Chihuly Glass Chandelier. Renowned glass artist Dale Chihuly created this serpentine green-and-blue masterpiece (in the main entrance) specifically for the V&A in 2001, when an exhibition of his work was staged in the museum's outdoor courtyard. The chandelier is 8m (26 ft.) tall and made up of thousands of exquisite hand-blown glass baubles. Despite its airy effect, it weighs 1.7 metric tons (3,750 lbs.). *Foyer.* ⏱ *3 min.*

❷ ★★★ kids The British Galleries. This stellar example of 21st-century curatorship features some of England's greatest cultural treasures. The big draw is the **Great Bed of Ware** (Room 57), a masterpiece of woodcarving mentioned in Shakespeare's *Twelfth Night.* Built around 1590 as a sales gimmick for an inn, the bed is now covered in I WAS HERE graffiti and wax seals left by centuries of visitors. Another highlight is the *Portrait of Margaret Layton* (Room 56). The painting of the early-17th-century noblewoman is rather ordinary, but the fine jacket embroidered with silver thread and colored silks displayed alongside it is the very one worn in the portrait. ⏱ *45 min.*

❸ ★★ Beasts of Dacre. These four heraldic animals (gryphon, bull, dolphin, and ram) were carved for the Dacres, one of northern England's most important families, in 1520. The wooden figures survived a fire in 1844, only to be restored in a rather gaudy, Victorian carousel style. *Stairway C.* ⏱ *5 min.*

❹ ★★★ Raphael's Cartoons. Dating back to 1521, these immense

Interior of the V&A Museum.

and expertly rendered drawings ("cartoon" is derived from the Italian word for a large piece of paper, *cartone*) were used by the artist Raphael to plot a set of tapestries intended to hang in Rome's Sistine Chapel. *Room 48a.* ⏱ *15 min.*

❺ ★★ kids Fashion Gallery. Reopened after a major refurbishment, this is part of the world's largest collection of clothing, featuring everything from the dandy regalia of 18th-century aristocrats to bizarre creations by such 21st-century designers as Vivienne Westwood. *Room 40.* ⏱ *25 min.*

❻ ★★★ Ironwork Gallery. Past the curlicued gates and nostalgic displays of cookie tins lining the museum's longest gallery, you'll find the stupendous **Hereford Screen,** a masterpiece of Victorian ironwork designed by the same man who devised the Albert

Memorial (p 39, **7**). Check out a bird's-eye view of the foyer's chandelier. *Room 114.* ⏱ *20 min.*

7 ★★★ **Medieval & Renaissance Galleries.** These galleries spread over three floors (0, 1, and 2) and aim to provide a complete overview of the progress of European art and culture from A.D. 300 to 1600; no mean ambition. The galleries comprise a mélange of tapestries, stained glass, statuary, glass, and metalwork. Notable items include Sir Paul Pindar's house, a rare wooden facade from a pre-Great Fire of London building; exhibits illustrating Donatello's revolution in sculpting stone (Room 64); and, in Room 64a, a densely packed notebook bursting with ideas from the mind of Leonardo da Vinci. ⏱ *40 min.*

8 ★★★ **kids Cast Courts.** These two popular rooms contain plaster-cast copies of some of the most famous European sculptures throughout history, including

Nineteenth-century plaster cast of Trajan's Column in the Cast Courts.

Trajan's Column from Ancient Rome (in two giant pieces), a version of Michelangelo's iconic Renaissance *David* (whose nudity so shocked Queen Victoria that she had a fig leaf made for it—it's now displayed behind the statue), and a copy of Ghiberti's famous bronze doors for Florence's Baptistery. *Rooms 46, 46a & 46b.* ⏱ *25 min.*

9 ★★ **Sculpture Galleries.** British garden and funerary sculptures from the 18th century fill rooms 22 to 24, joined by another couple of galleries (rooms 26 and 27) of religious sculptures and carvings. Produced in Western Europe between 1300 and 1600, the wooden figures were vividly painted, giving them an almost hyper-real appearance. ⏱ *20 min.*

10 ★★★ **Tippoo's Tiger.** Star of the South Asia Gallery—if not the entire V&A—is this once-animatronic, once-musical wooden tiger mauling a prone British soldier. It was commissioned for (and to represent) Tipu Sultan, ruler of Mysore, in 1793. Alas for him, things didn't quite work out as he planned: He was killed when his capital, Seringapatam, fell to soldiers of the British East India Company in 1799. They snatched the Tiger and shipped it to London. *Room 41.* ⏱ *10 min.*

For a quick outdoor snack, grab a table or recline in the **11** **kids** **John Madejski Garden.** The water jets are fun for kids; on a sunny day you may not want to go back inside. *Inner Courtyard. Open summer only. £.*

12 ★★ **The Ceramic Staircase.** The V&A's first director, Henry Cole, designed these stairs, intending to doll up all the museum's staircases

The V&A: Practical Matters

The Victoria & Albert Museum (☎ 020/7942-2000; vam.ac.uk/south-kensington) is located on Cromwell Road, at the corner of Exhibition Road. From South Kensington Tube Station, follow well-marked signs to the museum (5 min.).

Admission is free, except to special exhibitions (many of which are well worth seeing, with creative curation that justifies sometimes steep admission prices). The museum is open daily from 10am to 5:45pm. On Friday, the V&A stays open until 10pm. Free, volunteer-led Highlights and themed gallery tours run through the day; inquire at the desk when you arrive. On weekends and during school breaks, there are activities to engage kids of all ages; fun, self-guided trails are free to download at **vam.ac.uk/info/families**.

in this ceramics-gone-mad style. For better or worse, when costs spiraled out of control in 1870, the project was quietly dropped. *Staircase I.* ⏲ *10 min.*

⓭ ★★ **Gilbert Collection.** This shimmering array of gold jewelry, silvery statuary, mosaics, enamel portraits, and other historic *objets d'art* was put together by the British-born businessman Sir Arthur Gilbert and his wife Rosalinde, and donated to the nation in 1996. A 19th-century ceramic tabletop illustrating where to spend "24 Hours in Rome" is like an early travel guide. Stars of the show are the almost ridiculously opulent jewel-encrusted 18th-century snuffboxes; magnifying glasses are supplied for a close-up look. *Rooms 70–73.* ⏲ *25 min.*

⓮ ★★ **Silver Gallery.** This hall displays a dazzling (literally) array of some 10,000 silver objects from the past 600 years, ranging from baby rattles and candelabras to bath-size punch bowls. Highlights include a 15th-century German reliquary depicting an arrow-pierced St. Sebastian; Elizabethan gambling

counters; and ornate 17th-century Swedish drinking tankards. Interactive educational displays reveal some secrets of silver smithery. Keeping these rooms polished must be a full-time job. *Rooms 65–70a.* ⏲ *25 min.*

⓯ ★★ **Gilbert Bayes Sculpture Gallery.** This narrow gallery examines the craft of sculpture, showing each stage of the creative process with pieces selected from different eras to highlight the various techniques and materials (including stone, bronze, and ivory) used by sculptors. It also gives you a treetop view down into the Cast Courts. *Room 111.* ⏲ *20 min.*

The splendid ⓰ ★★★ **V&A Café** incorporates the original 19th-century Arts and Crafts refreshment rooms (the world's first museum restaurant) and is overlooked by stained glass and ornate ceramics and tiles. It's as much a sight as the museum's exhibits. The food served is acceptable and affordable hot English fare, plus sandwiches and salads. *Ground Level. £–££.*

Royal Westminster & Kensington

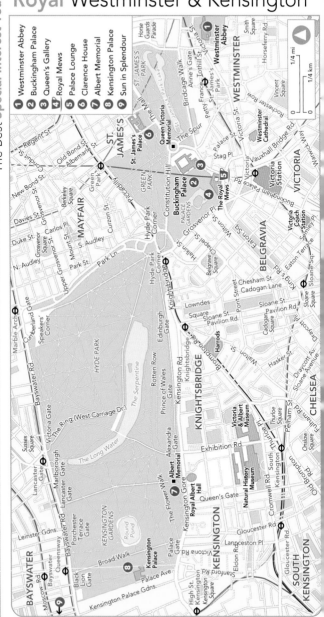

1 Westminster Abbey
2 Buckingham Palace
3 Queen's Gallery
4 Royal Mews
5 Palace Lounge
6 Clarence House
7 Albert Memorial
8 Kensington Palace
9 Sun in Splendour

The 2020s have been a lively decade for the British monarchy, whose public grief, pomp, and extravagant ceremony have been broadcast to every corner of the planet. The whole docusoap seems almost scripted for the entertainment of tourists, who never get enough of the riches, history, and gossip that have always defined royalty. This full-day tour serves up some of the city's royal highlights and a glimpse into the London lives of royals past and present. START: **Tube to Westminster.**

❶ ★★★ Westminster Abbey. It's impossible to overstate the significance of "the Abbey" in the history of British monarchy. William the Conqueror was crowned here (on Christmas Day, 1066), as was Charles III in 2023. Booking the first admission slot of the day is your best shot at some serenity around its majestic interior. ⏱ 1½ hr. See p 9, ❶.

❷ ★★ Buckingham Palace. Our tour continues at Buckingham Palace, the main residence of the monarch. The palace was originally built for the Duke of Buckingham and sold in 1761 to King George III (who needed the space for his 15 children). George IV had it remodeled by famed architect John Nash in the 1820s. For most of the year, you'll have to content yourself with views through the railings of its rather boxy exterior and **Changing the Guard** (p 21, ❷). However, for 10 weeks from mid-July to September, when the monarch is elsewhere, a few of the palace's lavish 500-plus rooms are opened up for guided tours, including 19 State Rooms, the Grand Staircase, and Throne Room. You can also take a walk across the famous palace garden. The palace has an aloofness that makes it difficult to love—even for royals, so they say—but it still provides an intriguing glimpse inside one of the gilded cages of British power. Book the earliest timed tour possible via the website to get the best price (listed below) and avoid the crowds. ⏱ 1½ hr. Buckingham Palace Rd. No phone. royalcollection.org.uk. Admission

Changing the Guard at Buckingham Palace.

(includes self-guided audio tour) £30 adults, £19.50 youths 18–24, £16.50 children 5–17, £77 family (2+2). Mid-July–Aug Thurs–Mon 9:30am–7:30pm (last admission 5:15pm), Sept closes 1 hr. earlier. Tube: Victoria, Green Park, or St. James's Park.

❸ ★★★ Queen's Gallery. This well-curated museum answers the question of how one furnishes and decorates a palace or two. Priceless treasures from the monarch's private collection of paintings, jewelry, furniture, and bibelots are displayed in sumptuous Georgian surroundings. The exhibits rotate (the family's holdings include, among other items, 10,000 Old Masters and enough *objets d'art* to fill several palaces—which they do, when they aren't here), but whatever is on display will be top-notch. You'll also find the city's best gift shop for royalty-related items, both affordable and budget-busting. ⏱ 1 hr. Buckingham Palace Rd. No phone. royalcollection.org.uk. £19 adults, £12 youths 18–24, £9.50 children 5–17. Thurs–Sun 10am–5:30pm (last admission 4:15pm). Closed for a few weeks when temporary exhibitions rotate in/out; check website for dates. Tube: Victoria or St. James's Park.

4 ★★ 🔵 **Royal Mews.** This oddly affecting royal experience is a great diversion if you're waiting for your timed entry slot to Buckingham Palace. Even if you're not into horses, you'll be fascinated by this peek into the lives of the King's privileged equines. The stalls at this working stable are roomy, the tack is pristine, and the ceremonial carriages (including the ornate **Gold State Coach**, used for the Coronation of Charles III, and the coach that both princesses Diana and Catherine rode in after their weddings to their princes) are eye-popping. A small exhibit tells you about the role royal horses have played in the past and present; old sepia-toned pictures show various royals and their four-footed friends. ⏱ 45 min. Buckingham Gate. No phone. royalcollection. org.uk. £15 adults, £10 youths 18–24, £9 children 5–17, £40 family (2+2). Mar–Oct Thurs–Mon 10am–5pm. Tube: Victoria or St. James's Park.

Coronation Coach at the Royal Mews.

Overlooking the entrance to the Royal Mews is the **5** ★ **Palace Lounge,** an atmospheric spot to take a refined afternoon tea (£70 per adult, kids' tea £35) or a light meal. You may get a glimpse of deliveries being made to Buckingham Palace in old-fashioned wagons. You'll need to give 24 hours' notice for gluten-free, vegetarian, or vegan teas. *Inside Rubens at the Palace Hotel, 39 Buckingham Palace Rd. No phone. rubenshotel.com. ££.*

6 ★ **Clarence House.** The list of former inhabitants of this rather staid mansion reads like a who's who of recent royals. It was designed in the 1820s by John Nash, the Royal Family's then favorite architect, for the Duke of Clarence, who continued residing there during his brief 7-year reign as William IV. In 1947 it was home to Princess Elizabeth following her marriage to Prince Philip. Before she succeeded to the throne she had given way to her mother, the "Queen Mother," who lived here until her death in 2002. It was the official residence of Prince Charles and the Duchess of Cornwall before they became Charles III and Queen

Tea at Palace Lounge.

Camilla. In August (usually) visitors can take a guided tour of state rooms, where a good deal of the royal art and furniture collection is displayed. Despite this, Clarence House is an essential tourism stop for committed royal-watchers only. It's a 40-minute walk through parks (mostly) from here to the next stop; for the footsore, take bus 9 from Piccadilly, opposite Green Park Station, towards Hammersmith, and get off at the Royal Albert Hall (20 min.). ⏱ *45 min. St. James's Palace, The Mall. No phone. royalcollection.org. uk. £10.30 adults, £6.20 children 5–16. Aug Mon–Fri 10am–4:30pm, Sat–Sun 10am–5:30pm. Tube: Green Park.*

⑦ ★ kids Albert Memorial. An inconsolable Queen Victoria spent an obscene amount of public money on this 55m-tall (180 ft.) gaudy neo-Gothic shrine to her husband, Albert, who died of typhoid fever in 1861. The project (completed in 1876) didn't go down too well with her ministers, but Victoria was not a woman to whom one said no. The excessively ornate mass of gilt, marble, statuary, and mosaics stands in all its dubious glory across the street from the equally fabulous (and much more useful) **Royal Albert Hall.** The book Albert is holding is a catalogue from the Great Exhibition, of which he was patron. The Great Exhibition formed the seed from which grew the great museums of South Kensington. ⏱ *10 min. Kensington Gardens (west of Exhibition Rd.). Free admission. Tube: S. Kensington.*

⑧ ★★★ kids Kensington Palace. A royal palace since the late 17th century, when the original Jacobean mansion was given a thorough makeover by Sir Christopher Wren for the new king, William III, this provides a much more satisfying visit than Buckingham Palace (and it's open most of the year). The palace is smaller, and curators go out of their way to entertain and inform visitors. Following its most significant revamp in more than a century, palace gardens are now connected to Kensington Gardens for the first time since the 19th century. The King's (George II, patron of the composer Handel) and Queen's State Apartments have been "reimagined" elegantly, including with multimedia installations, theatrical exhibits, and items from the Royal Ceremonial Dress Collection. Themes and installations change every year, and have at times covered the lives of late-17th- and early-18th-century queens Mary II and Anne, and of course, Victoria. The palace is now the official residence of the Prince and Princess of Wales. ⏱ *2 hr. Kensington Gardens.* ☎ *0333/320-6000. hrp.org.uk/ kensington-palace. £25 adults, £20 seniors & students, £13 children 5–15. Wed–Sun 10am–6pm (Nov–Feb 10am–4pm). Tube: High St. Kensington or Queensway.*

If you have any energy left—or are heading to Notting Hill to shop or dine—a 15-minute walk takes you to the **⑨ ☕ ★★ Sun in Splendour,** my favorite Portobello Road watering hole. You can't miss the canary-yellow building, where many a shopper begins or ends their day at the famous street market (p 96). *7 Portobello Rd.* ☎ *020/7792-0914. suninsplendourpub.co.uk. £.*

Art Lovers' London

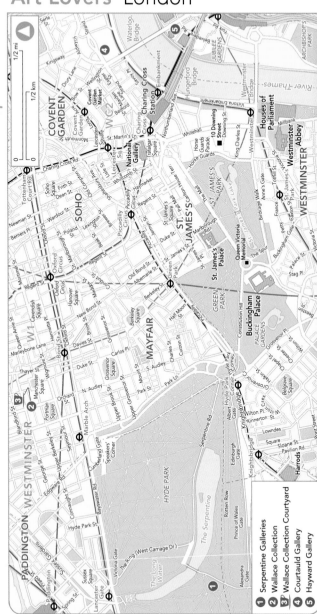

1 Serpentine Galleries
2 Wallace Collection
3 Wallace Collection Courtyard
4 Courtauld Gallery
5 Hayward Gallery

Gems aplenty are stashed in museums and galleries away from the main tourist trail. This tour visits eras and genres that showcase the diversity of London's art world—and yet, somehow, still only scratches the surface: Check arts pages to see what's on when you're in town. And before you go anywhere, download the **Bloomberg Connects** app for free audio and other guides to many London art spaces. START: **Tube to Lancaster Gate.**

① ★★ Serpentine Galleries.

Twin sites in the middle of Hyde Park host anything-goes contemporary shows, from experimental video game art to plain old painting. Highlight of the year for the Serpentine South—which began life as a 1930s tearoom—is its Summer Pavilion. Each year since 2000 a renowned architect has been commissioned to build a Pavilion in the gallery garden. It must be their first complete structure in England. Alumni include the likes of Frank Gehry, Zaha Hadid, and Lina Ghotmeh. ⏱ 1 hr. Kensington Gardens. ☎ 020/7402-6075. serpentine galleries.org. Free admission. Tues–Sun 10am–6pm. Tube: Lancaster Gate.

② ★★★ Wallace Collection.

Left to the nation in 1897, this collection offers an astonishing glimpse into the buying power of the English gentry following the French Revolution, when important art was made instantly homeless by the guillotine. Paintings are outstanding, with works by Titian and Canaletto; and a Dutch collection with Rembrandt and Hals' famous Laughing Cavalier. The museum also has Sèvres porcelain and an array of European and Asian arms and armor—works of art in their own right. ⏱ 1¾ hr. Hertford House, Manchester Sq. ☎ 020/7563-9500. wallacecollection.org. Free admission, except for some temporary exhibitions. Daily 10am–5pm. Free tour of highlights at 2:30pm. Tube: Bond St.

The ③ ★★ Wallace Collection Courtyard is a contemplative spot to pause. Choose coffee and snacks or a French brasserie-style restaurant, both al fresco but protected against the elements. Hertford House, Manchester Sq. ☎ 020/7563-9500. £–££.

④ ★★★ Courtauld Gallery.

Why pay to see art when so many great paintings in London are free to view? Well, this place is a bit special. In a handful of top-floor rooms you can trace the story of French Impressionism from early works (Manet's Folies-Bergère

Decorative arts admirer at the Wallace Collection.

Vincent Van Gogh self-portrait at the Courtauld Gallery.

masterpiece, Renoir, Degas' dancers) through High Impressionist works by Pissarro and Monet to Post-Impressionist masterpieces of Cézanne and Bonnard. The rest of this focused collection, especially Italian and Flemish Renaissance art, is also excellent. But there's no competing with those. ⏱ *1½ hr. Somerset House, Strand.* ☎ *020/3947-7777. courtauld.ac.uk/gallery. £10 adults (£12 on weekends), free students & children 18 and under. Daily 10am–5:15pm. Tube: Temple.*

⑤ ★★ Hayward Gallery. Amid the Brutalist architecture of the South Bank Centre—you either love it or hate it—the Hayward is one of London's major contemporary art spaces, with both indoor and outdoor exhibits. Zeitgeisty shows often break new ground or offer a retrospective for a major contemporary artist. ⏱ *1¼ hr. Belvedere Rd.* ☎ *020/3879-9555. southbank centre.co.uk. Main exhibitions around £16 (off-peak discounts for visitors under 30); also free shows always available. Wed–Sun 10am–6pm (Sat until 8pm). Tube: Waterloo.*

Hayward Gallery.

Kids' London

KENSINGTON
GARDENS

Round
Pond

HYDE PARK

The Serpentine

0 — 1/2 mi
0 — 1/2 km

Serpentine Rd.

Rotten Row

The Flower Walk

❹

Queen's
Gate
Kensington Gore

■ Albert
Memorial

Alexandra
Gate

Prince of Wales
Gate

Edinburgh
Gate

Albert Hyde Park
Gate Corner

Hyde Park
Corner

Knightsbridge

Prince Consort Rd.

Royal Albert
Hall

KNIGHTSBRIDGE

Kensington Rd.

Knightsbridge

Lowndes
St.

Wilton
Cres.

Halkin St.

Belgrave
Square

Belgrave Chapel St.

Science
Museum

❶

Elvaston Place

Queen's Gate Pl.

Natural History
Museum

❸

Exhibition Rd.

Cheval Pl.

Brompton Rd.

Victoria
& Victoria
Museum

Beauchamp Pl.

Harrods

Hans Cr.

Sloane St.

Pavilion Rd.

Pont Street

Cadogan Place

Eaton Sq.

Eaton Pl.

BELGRAVIA

Gloucester Rd.

Cromwell Rd.

South
Kensington

Thurloe Pl.

Thurloe
Square

Cadogan Sq.

Sloane St.

Milner St.

Pavilion Rd.

King's Rd.

Eaton Terrace

Queen Elizabeth St.

Ebury St.

Harrington Rd.

Pelham St.

Pelham
Crescent

Ixworth Place

Hasker St.

Draycott Av.

Sloane Avenue

Sloane St.

Sloane
Square

Sloane Sq.

Old Brompton Rd.

Onslow Gardens

Onslow
Square

Sumner Pl.

Fulham Rd.

Cale St.

Elystan St.

Draycott Pl.

Elystan Place

SOUTH
KENSINGTON

The
Boltons

Sydney St.

Dovehouse St.

Astell St.

King's Rd.

Chelsea
Square

CHELSEA

❶ Science Museum
❷ Kensington Creperie
❸ Natural History Museum
❹ Kensington Gardens

London is one of Europe's top urban playgrounds for kids. Nearly all major museums have well-thought-out trails and activities to entertain or inspire, and to show off the collections in ways kids of any age can appreciate. Some museums have dedicated apps; and our favorites are curated with kids in mind… and completely free. START: **Tube to South Kensington.**

❶ ★★★ kids **Science Museum.** Packed with hands-on fun, this London institution appeals to children (and adults) of all ages, with seven levels of exhibits tracing the progress of technology and supplying buttons to press and levers to pull along the way. Dedicated sections for kids include the **Garden,** an interactive play area for 3- to 6-year-olds, and **Wonderlab,** with more than 50 hands-on experiments. The museum stages numerous free events for children and

offers daily tours of galleries and an IMAX cinema. Plus, the gift shop is almost as interesting as the exhibits. Prebooking a timed admission slot to the museum is compulsory; go as early as your children can be persuaded to avoid the crowds. ⏱ *2 hr. Exhibition Rd.* ☎ *033/0058-0058. sciencemuseum.org.uk. Free admission, except for special exhibitions/experiences, IMAX & Wonderlab (£11, £9 children). Daily 10am–6pm. Tube: S. Kensington.*

2 ★ kids **Kensington Creperie.** The museum cafes are fine, but I suggest a break from museumland at this fun French crêperie a couple minutes' walk away. It serves sweet and savory crêpes or galettes (types of thin pancake), fresh waffles, and ice cream. *2 Exhibition Rd.* ☎ *020/7589-8947. kensington creperie.com. £–££.*

3 ★★★ kids **Natural History Museum.** This museum's 19th-century building alone is worth a look, with relief statues of beasts incorporated into its terracotta facade; it's been a favorite of movie-makers from *One of Our Dinosaurs is Missing* (1975) to the 21st-century *Paddington* films. Although not as edgy as the Science Museum next door, this collection is no fossil. Exhibits include a growling, prowling T. rex and other animatronic beasts, an interactive rainforest, an earthquake simulator, and topnotch mineral and meteorite displays. The old animal dioramas are still around, but the Darwin Centre's 8-story **Cocoon** has left them in the dust; highlights include audiovisual shows and interactive events with naturalists and photographers (not to mention 28 million insects and 6 million plant specimens). **Note:** Any line is almost always shorter if you

Exploring the Natural History Museum.

use the side entrance on Exhibition Road. ⏲ *1½ hr. Cromwell Rd. (at Exhibition Rd.).* ☎ *020/7942-5000. nhm.ac.uk. Free admission, except for temporary exhibits. Daily 10am–5:50pm. Tube: S. Kensington.*

4 ★★★ kids **Kensington Gardens.** It's less than 10 minutes' walk to a vast green space where youngsters can cut loose—or snooze under a tree. *See* *p 100,* **9**.

Hampton Court Palace

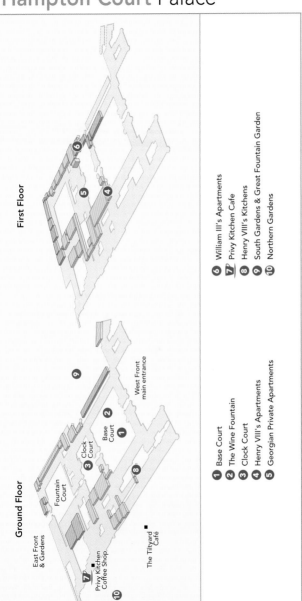

Ground Floor

First Floor

East Front & Gardens

Fountain Court

Clock Court

Base Court

West Front main entrance

Privy Kitchen Coffee Shop

The Tiltyard Café

1 Base Court
2 The Wine Fountain
3 Clock Court
4 Henry VIII's Apartments
5 Georgian Private Apartments

6 William III's Apartments
7 Privy Kitchen Cafe
8 Henry VIII's Kitchens
9 South Gardens & Great Fountain Garden
10 Northern Gardens

This Tudor masterpiece was built by Cardinal Thomas Wolsey in 1514, only to be snatched up by Henry VIII (r. 1509–47) when Wolsey fell out of favor for failing to secure the Pope's permission for Henry's (first) divorce. Encompassing some 1,500 rooms (about 70 are open to visitors) and 500 miles of corridors, it's one of the biggest palaces ever built and served as a royal residence from 1528 to 1737. Here you can tread the same paths as Elizabeth I, William III, and George II as you learn about court life through the centuries. START: **Train or riverboat to Hampton Court.**

❶ ★★ Base Court. Monarchs arrived at Hampton Court on the River Thames and entered via the South Gardens (**❾**). Visitors today, however, pass through a gatehouse built by Henry VIII for the common folk, and into this Tudor-style courtyard, which is almost exactly as it was when Cardinal Wolsey commissioned it in 1515. ⏱ *10 min.*

❷ ★ The Wine Fountain. In 2010 a replica wine fountain was built over the foundations of a Tudor original, previously on the south side of the Base Court. The design is based on a representation of the *Field of the Cloth of Gold* painting, which hangs inside the palace. For most of the year the 4m (13-ft.) high fountain, adorned with 40 gilded lions' heads, pours water from eight taps, but it has been adapted to occasionally serve something stronger—just as in Henry's day. ⏱ *5 min.*

❸ ★★ Clock Court. From Base Court, pass through the **Anne Boleyn Gatehouse** (built in the 1800s, centuries after the beheaded queen's execution) and into Clock Court, which encompasses several architectural styles, ranging from Tudor (the north side) to 18th-century Gothic (the east side). Its major attraction is the elaborate **Astronomical Clock,** built for Henry VIII. Note the sun revolving around the Earth—the clock was built before Galileo and Copernicus debunked that myth. ⏱ *10 min.*

❹ ★★★ Henry VIII's Apartments. Even though Sir Christopher Wren modified some of them, these rooms remain best examples of Tudor style in England. Don't miss the elaborately gilded ceiling of the **Chapel Royal,** a still-functioning royal church where Henry was informed of the "misconduct" of his adulterous fifth wife, Catherine

Hampton Court Palace.

One of Hampton Court's many kitchens.

Howard, and later married wife number six, Catherine Parr. An exact replica of Henry's crown is displayed on the Royal Pew. Just off the chapel is the **Haunted Gallery,** where Howard's specter reportedly still pleads for her life (though if you believe the many ghost stories, this "Haunted Gallery" may be one of the least haunted rooms in the whole palace). The **Watching Chamber,** where senior courtiers would dine, is the only one of Henry VIII's many English estate rooms in something close to its original form (the fireplace and stained glass are not originals). Also impressive is the **Great Hall,** with a set of tapestries (real gold and silver thread) that cost Henry as much as his naval fleet. ⏱ *50 min.*

⑤ ★★ Georgian Story. The private apartments of George II and Queen Caroline still look as they did in 1737, when Caroline died and the royal court left this palace forever. (When George was Prince of Wales, these same rooms witnessed a father/son struggle for popularity and influence that remains notorious in royal history.) The **Presence Chamber** of the 10-year-old Duke of Cumberland (George's second son) is the only room at the palace that's fully paneled, gilded, and painted. A portion of the ceiling of the **Wolsey Closet** survives from the Tudor era, with the rest decorated in the Renaissance style. The state bed in the **Queen's Bedchamber** is a

reproduction. If the king and queen wanted to sleep together in privacy (no mean feat for the royal couple), it was to this room they retired, thanks to a rather sophisticated door lock. ⏱ *45 min.*

⑥ ★★★ William III's Apartments. These baroque rooms (among the finest of their kind) were designed by Sir Christopher Wren for William III (r. 1689–1702), who did more to shape the palace than any other monarch, although he died shortly after moving in. The apartments were badly damaged in a 1986 fire but have been fully restored. All the rooms in this wing are impressive, notably the **King's Guard Chamber,** with a spectacular collection of nearly 3,000 weapons mounted on its walls. The **Presence Chamber** has an exquisite rock-crystal chandelier; the **Great Bedchamber** (ceremonial only—the king slept elsewhere) is loaded with gilded furniture, priceless tapestries, and a magnificent red-velvet canopy bed; and the relatively snug **Private Dining Room** has a reproduction of the king's gold-plated dining service. ⏱ *1 hr.*

The **⑦ ★ kids Privy Kitchen Cafe** has a real Tudor atmosphere—original kitchens with wooden tables, flagstones, and 16th-century-style chandeliers—along with decent pastries, light lunches, and afternoon tea. £.

A live interpreter in the role of Henry VIII, wearing a re-created version of the king's Crown of State.

❽ ★★★ Henry VIII's Kitchens. At its peak, Hampton Court's kitchen staff catered two meals a day to a household of 600—more than almost any modern hotel. An enormous effort of labor prepared and served up some 8,200 sheep, 1,240 oxen, and 600,000 gallons of beer a year. Once the palace lost its popularity with the royal set, these 50-room kitchens were converted into apartments. They were restored authentically in 1991. ⏱ *45 min.*

❾ ★★★ The South Gardens & Great Fountain Garden. The palace's southern gardens are home to William III's **Privy Garden,** with its elaborate baroque ironwork screen; the box-hedged **Knot Garden,** which resembles a traditional Tudor garden; and the lovely sunken **Pond Gardens.** The **Great Vine** is one of the oldest (planted in 1768) and largest grape vines in the world. Its annual 270kg (600 lb.) crop is sold in the palace shops after the August Bank Holiday. The **Orangery** displays Mantegna's nine-painting masterpiece, *Triumphs of Caesar,* an important work of the Italian Renaissance. ⏱ *50 min.*

❿ ★★★ kids The Northern Gardens. Renowned for their spring bulbs and **Rose Garden** (blooms peak in June), the Northern Gardens are where you'll find the world's most famous **Hedge Maze,** whose labyrinthine paths cover nearly a half-mile. Planted in 1702, the maze has trapped many a visitor in its clutches. When you do escape, stroll to the adjacent **Tiltyard** (jousting area), where you'll find several walled gardens, as well as the only surviving tiltyard tower (used to seat spectators at tournaments) built for Henry VIII. ⏱ *45 min.*

Practical Matters: Hampton Court

Hampton Court Palace is in East Molesey, Surrey, 13 miles west of Central London. Trains from London Waterloo Station to Hampton Court take 35 minutes; when you exit the station, turn right and follow the signs to the palace, a 5-minute walk away. The cheapest way to pay is with Oyster (£5, or £8 peak fare on weekday morning and evening rush hours), rather than buying a separate train ticket. Admission to the palace and gardens costs £26 adults, £13 children aged 5 to 15, £11 seniors and students (a couple of pounds per person more expensive on weekends). To be sure of entry, book tickets in advance (even the same day) at **hrp.org.uk/hampton-court-palace**. Admission includes a self-guided audio tour; collect it at the information center off Base Court (❶). In July and August, the palace is open daily from 10am to 5:30pm; otherwise, it opens Wednesday through Sunday only.

Literary London

1. Temple Church
2. Dr. Johnson's House
3. Charles Dickens Museum
4. Platform 9 ¾
5. British Library
6. 50 Gordon Square
7. Senate House
8. Fitzroy Tavern

From Shakespeare premiering plays at the Globe to Dickens illuminating the plight of the backstreet poor, London and literature have long gone together like a good book and a comfy armchair. This tour takes you to sites associated with the city's most illustrious writers, as well as places where you can take a closer look at the works themselves. Wear comfortable shoes: There's a fair bit of walking. START: **Tube to Temple.**

❶ ★★ Temple Church. Its pivotal plot role in *The Da Vinci Code*, the biggest-selling non-wizarding English language book of the 21st century, saw this Gothic church enjoy a huge spike in visitor numbers. It was built for the Knights Templar in the 1100s, a group of warrior priests who fought in the Crusades. The distinctive circular nave is based on the Church of the Holy Sepulcher in Jerusalem. Within are effigy tombs of various crusaders. ⏱ *30 min. King's Bench Walk.* ☎ *020/7353-3470. templechurch.com. £5 adults, £3 seniors & students, free children 16 & under. Mon–Fri 10am–4pm; check website for any weekend opening dates. Tube: Temple or Blackfriars.*

❷ ★★ Dr. Johnson's House. Travel writers have long been grateful to Dr. Samuel Johnson. His proud maxim, "When a man is tired of London, he is tired of life…," has kicked off many an introduction to the city. But Johnson was more than a mere quotation machine. One of the great scholars of the 18th century, he was also a poet, a biographer, a critic, and the compiler of one of the first and most influential English-language dictionaries. He worked on his mighty tome over a period of 9 years at his Queen Anne home, which has been restored to its mid-18th-century prime and is filled with Johnson-related paraphernalia. A bronze of Johnson's cat Hodge—"a very fine

A grotesque on the façade of Temple Church.

cat indeed"—faces his old home across Gough Square. ⏱ *30 min. 17 Gough Sq.* ☎ *020/7353-3745. drjohnsonshouse.org. £9 adults, £8 seniors, £4 children 5–17. Mon & Thurs–Sat 11am–5pm. Tube: Chancery Lane or Blackfriars.*

❸ ★★ Charles Dickens Museum. Dickens lived (and lodged) all over the city, but this museum occupies the only London home of the great Victorian novelist that is still standing. He lived here only from 1837 to 1840, but this being Dickens, that was more than enough time to churn out some sizeable classics, including *Nicholas Nickleby* and *Oliver Twist*. The rooms have been restored in period style and adorned with various mementos from his life, including a number of original manuscripts and his (presumably reinforced) quill pen. ① *1 hr. 48–49 Doughty St.* ☎ *020/7405-2127. dickensmuseum. com. £12.50 adults, £10.50 seniors & students, £7.50 children 6–16. Wed–Sun 10am–5pm. Tube: Russell Sq.*

④ ★ kids **Platform 9¾.** All aboard the Hogwarts Express! J.K. Rowling's famous fictional train departure point, Platform 9¾, has been brought to (sort of) life at King's Cross Station in the form of a sign and a luggage trolley seemingly stuck halfway through a wall, as if magically passing through. Cameras at the ready! There is (of course) a Harry Potter merch shop right beside it—and a seemingly 24/7 line for a selfie. ① *10 min. Western Departures Concourse,* *King's Cross Station, Euston Rd. harrypottershop.co.uk. Tube: King's Cross.*

⑤ ★★★ kids **British Library.** As the ultimate repository of British literature, the B.L. receives a copy of every single book published in the U.K., amounting to some 14 million volumes stored on 400 miles of bookshelves (largely below-ground). The library's current home may be less elegant than its predecessor at the British Museum (p 28), but it's much more user-friendly. What's on display at the free "Treasures of the British Library" exhibition is constantly rotated, but you will certainly see some of the most precious possessions, such as Shakespeare's *First Folio*, Brontë manuscripts, notebooks scribbled in by Leonardo da Vinci, or Lewis Carroll's diary. The paid temporary exhibitions are usually worth checking out, too. ① *1 hr. 96 Euston Rd.* ☎ *01937/546-546. bl.uk. Free admission. Mon–Thurs*

The Charles Dickens Museum.

9:30am–8pm, Fri 9:30am–6pm, Sat 9:30am–5pm, Sun 11am–5pm. Tube: King's Cross.

6 ★ 50 Gordon Square. A brown plaque marks the headquarters of the Bloomsbury Group, a collective of writers, artists, and economists, including Virginia Woolf, E. M. Forster, and John Maynard Keynes, who met here in the early 20th century, when Bloomsbury was the unofficial capital of literary London.

7 ★ Senate House. Exit the southwest corner of Gordon Square and to the south you'll see a sinister-looking, vaguely pyramidal building with long, narrow windows. This is Senate House, the

inspiration for the "Ministry of Truth" in George Orwell's *1984,* and where Orwell's wife, Evelyn Waugh, and Dorothy L. Sayers worked during World War II. It's now part of the University of London. *Malet St.*

Between the 1920s and 1950s **8** **★★ The Fitzroy Tavern** was a noted boozy hangout for writers including George Orwell and Dylan Thomas (there's a picture on the wall of Thomas drinking in the pub). This Victorian original, complete with wooden screens and etched glass, is now owned by Sam Smith's Brewery and serves reasonably priced drinks and simple pub food. *16 Charlotte St.* ☎ *020/7580-3714. £.* ●

Chelsea

Natural History Museum

Victoria & Albert Museum

KNIGHTSBRIDGE

Queen's Gate

Cromwell Rd.

Cromwell Rd.

Thurloe Pl.

Brompton Rd.

Egerton Gdns

Thurloe Square

Harrington Rd.

South Kensington

Pelham St.

Draycott Av.

Sloane Avenue

SOUTH KENSINGTON

Old Brompton Rd.

Gardens

Onslow Gardens

Pelham Crescent

Ixworth Place

Elystan St.

Leicester Rd.

Onslow

Summer Pl.

Onslow Square

Fulham Rd.

Cale St.

Astell St.

CHELSEA

Roland Gardens

Gardens

Old Church St.

Chelsea Square

Dovehouse St.

Sydney St.

Flood St.

Drayton

Giston Rd.

Elm Park

Beaufort St.

Glebe Pl.

Oakley St.

Chelsea Manor St.

Limerston St.

Park Walk

King's Rd.

Old Church St.

Upper Cheyne Row

Cheyne Row

21

20

15

Cheyne

17

Cheyne Walk

Beaufort St.

19 **18**

Albert Bridge

16

Edith Grove

Cheyne Walk

Battersea Bridge

Battersea Bridge Rd.

BATTERSEA

0		1/4 mi
0		1/4 km

Previous page: On Lovat Lane in The City, old and new collide.

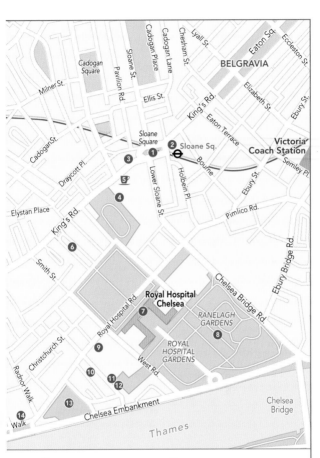

1 Sloane Square
2 Royal Court Theatre
3 King's Road
4 Saatchi Gallery
5 Polpo
6 Royal Avenue
7 Royal Hospital Chelsea
8 Ranelagh Gardens
9 National Army Museum
10 Oscar Wilde's Home
11 John Singer Sargent's Home
12 Augustus John's Studio
13 Chelsea Physic Garden
14 George Eliot's Home
15 Dante Gabriel Rossetti's Home
16 Albert Bridge
17 Carlyle Mansions
18 Statue of Sir Thomas More
19 Chelsea Old Church
20 Thomas Carlyle's House
21 Leigh Hunt's Home

Since the 16th century, when Henry VIII and Thomas More built country manors on its riverbanks, Chelsea has had a tradition of eccentricity, aristocracy, and artisanship. This now-posh district is great for a half-day stroll. Keep an eye peeled for blue plaques affixed to houses; they reveal the many historical figures who once called this neighborhood home. START: **Tube to Sloane Square.**

Sloane Square.

① Sloane Square. Royal physician Sir Hans Sloane (1660–1753), who helped found the British Museum, is the namesake of this busy square, marking the boundary between two well-to-do districts, Chelsea and Belgravia. In addition to his educational and medical achievements, Sloane discovered the milk-chocolate recipe that became the basis of the Cadbury chocolate empire. *Intersection of Sloane St. & King's Rd.*

② ★★ Royal Court Theatre. This restored theatre, originally built in 1888, is famed for showcasing playwrights such as George Bernard Shaw, John Osborne, and Harold Pinter. Nowadays, the work of today's most promising dramatists is performed on the two stages. *Sloane Sq.* ☎ *020/7565-5000. royalcourttheatre.com.*

③ ★★ King's Road. Chelsea's main road was once an exclusive royal passage used by King Charles II to travel between Whitehall and Hampton Court. It was also a favorite route of highwaymen looking to "liberate" royal goods. An echo of these King's Road robbers can be found in the prices of its chichi stores. These boutiques once helped the 1960s swing and '70s punks look the part, and today they attracts free-spending members of London's upper social strata. *Runs from Sloane Sq. southwest to Putney Bridge.*

④ ★★ Saatchi Gallery. The capital's largest contemporary art gallery was the brainchild of ad mogul and mega-collector Charles Saatchi. It rose to prominence championing the Young British Artists of the early 1990s—Damien Hirst, Tracy Emin et al.—and still lays on temporary exhibitions dedicated to all that's most challenging in the art world. Whatever's on display when you visit, it's liable to be controversial—or else the gallery isn't doing its job. ⓛ *50 min. Duke of York's Headquarters, King's Rd. saatchigallery.com. Exhibition tickets from free to £16. Daily 10am–6pm.*

Duke of York Square has chain dining spots galore, but you won't go wrong at **⑤ ★ Polpo.** A stylized London take on a Venetian bàcaro, it serves tapaslike small plates for brunch, lunch, or dinner appetites. *81 Duke of York Sq.* ☎ *020/7730-8900, polpo.co.uk. ££.*

⑥ ★ Royal Avenue. This short, picturesque road was not quite what William III intended in the 1690s. He wanted it to run all the way from

Polpo restaurant in Duke of York Square.

the nearby Chelsea Royal Hospital to Kensington Palace, but construction was cut short after his death. Still, it proved just the ticket for its most famous fictional resident, Ian Fleming's James Bond. *Between St. Leonard's Terrace & King's Rd.*

7 ★★ Royal Hospital Chelsea. This Christopher Wren masterpiece, commissioned by Charles II in 1686 as a retirement estate for injured and old soldiers, is still home to 400-plus "Chelsea Pensioners," who dress in traditional red uniforms and offer informative tours of the historic grounds, small museum, and chapel. Hospital grounds host the prestigious Chelsea Flower Show, held almost every May since 1912. ○ *1 hr. Royal Hospital Rd.* ☎ *020/7881-5237. chelsea-pensioners.co.uk. £15 guided tour (must be booked at least 1 month in advance). Chapel services open to public, Sun 9am & 11am.*

8 ★ Ranelagh Gardens. Once centered round a large rotunda (demolished in 1805), these gardens (some of the prettiest in London) were a favorite of 18th-century socialites who were occasionally entertained here by a young Mozart. *Behind Royal Hospital.*

9 ★★ kids National Army Museum. Home to the Duke of Wellington's shaving mirror and Florence Nightingale's lamp, plus plenty of assorted weaponry, this museum follows the history of Britain's land-fighting forces from 1066 to the present. A tank parked outside is the giveaway. ○ *45 min. Royal Hospital Rd. nam.ac.uk. Free admission. Tues–Sun 10am–5:30pm.*

10 ★ Oscar Wilde's Home. The eccentricities of Oscar and his wife, Constance (they lived here from 1885–95), were well known to neighbors, who would often see them on the street dressed in velvet (him) and a huge Gainsborough hat (her). Street boys would shout, "'Ere comes 'Amlet and Ophelia!" The house is not open to the public but is marked with a blue plaque. *34 Tite St.*

11 ★ John Singer Sargent's Home. The renowned American portraitist of the high and mighty lived and worked at this address (the former abode of equally famous James McNeill Whistler) from 1901 until his death in 1925. *31 Tite St.*

12 Augustus John's Studio. A renowned Welsh painter (1878–1961), John was one of Chelsea's most illustrious artists. His insightful portraits and landscapes made him famous, while his bohemian lifestyle and love affairs (including one with the mother

A toy display at the National Army Museum.

of James Bond creator Ian Fleming) earned him notoriety. *33 Tite St.*

⑬ ★★ Chelsea Physic Garden. This garden was established right here in 1673 by the Apothecaries' Company to cultivate medicinal plants and herbs—the only botanical garden of its type in the world. An international seed exchange program was begun in 1682 and continues to this day: Cotton seeds from the garden were sent to America in 1732, and slavery was their eventual harvest. ⏱ *45 min. 66 Royal Hospital Rd.* ☎ *020/7352-5646. chelseaphysicgarden.co.uk. £12.50 adults, £5 children 5–18, £37 family (2+3). Apr–Oct Sun–Fri 11–5pm; winter Mon–Fri 11am–3pm.*

⑭ George Eliot's Home. The famous Victorian novelist, born Mary Ann Evans in 1819, moved into this house with her new and much younger husband, John Cross, only a few months before her death in December 1880. *4 Cheyne Walk.*

⑮ Dante Gabriel Rossetti's Home. The eccentric Pre-Raphaelite poet and painter (1828–82) lived here after the death of his wife in 1862. He kept a menagerie of exotic animals, including kangaroos, a white bull, peacocks, and a wombat that inspired his friend, Lewis Carroll, to create the Dormouse for *Alice in Wonderland. 16 Cheyne Walk.*

⑯ ★★ Albert Bridge. Designed by R. M. Ordish, this picturesque suspension bridge linking Battersea and Chelsea was completed in 1873. Conservationists saved the bridge from destruction in the 1950s. In 1973, the cast-iron structure had new supports installed so it could cope with the rigors of modern traffic, yet it still tends to shake when things get busy (hence its nickname, the "Trembling Lady"). At night 4,000 bulbs light the way.

⑰ Carlyle Mansions. Over the past century or so, this redbrick apartment complex has been home to Henry James (1843–1916), who breathed his last here, T. S. Eliot (1888–1965), Ian Fleming (1908–1964), and Somerset Maugham (1874–1965)—fully earning its nickname: "The Writers' Block." *Cheyne Walk.*

⑱ ★ Statue of Sir Thomas More. Despite his long friendship with Henry VIII, Lord Chancellor Thomas More (1478–1535) refused to accept Henry as head of the Church of England after the king's notorious break with the Roman Catholic Church. More, who also wrote the philosophical work *Utopia*, paid for his religious conviction with his life: He was tried and subsequently beheaded for treason at

Albert Bridge.

the Tower of London. In 1935, the Pope Pius XI canonized him as the patron saint of lawyers and politicians. This statue of More, with its slightly odd gilded face, was erected outside Chelsea Old Church in 1969. *Old Church St.*

⑲ ★ **Chelsea Old Church.** A church has stood on this site since 1157. Although the structure suffered serious damage during the Blitz, it has since been rebuilt and restored. Sir Thomas More worshiped here (he built the South Chapel in 1528), and it was the setting for Henry VIII's secret marriage to third wife Jane Seymour in 1536. ① *15 min. 64 Cheyne Walk.* ☎ *020/7795-1019. chelseaoldchurch.org.uk. Free admission. Tues–Thurs 2–4pm.*

⑳ ★★ **Thomas Carlyle's House.** The famous Scottish historian (1795–1881) and his wife, Jane, entertained their friends Dickens and Chopin here. It was in this remarkably well-preserved Victorian home that the "Sage of Chelsea" finished his landmark *History of the French Revolution.* ① *30 min. 24 Cheyne Row.* ☎ *020/7352-5108. nationaltrust.org.uk/carlyles-house. £9 adults, £4.50 children 5–16. Mar–Oct Wed 11am–4:30pm.*

㉑ **Leigh Hunt's Home.** From 1833 to 1840, the noted poet and essayist (a friend of Byron and Keats) lived here and was well known for pestering neighbors for loans. His wife infuriated Jane Carlyle, the celebrated Victorian letter writer and wife of historian Thomas, by incessantly borrowing household items. *22 Upper Cheyne Row.*

Statue of Sir Thomas More.

Royal Greenwich

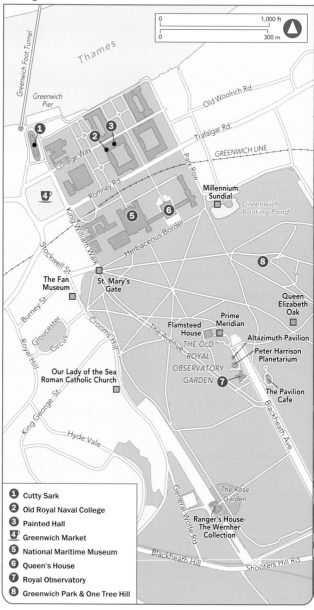

| 0 | | 1,000 ft |
| 0 | | 300 m |

1. Cutty Sark
2. Old Royal Naval College
3. Painted Hall
4. Greenwich Market
5. National Maritime Museum
6. Queen's House
7. Royal Observatory
8. Greenwich Park & One Tree Hill

Sorry, Manhattan: This is the OG Greenwich, birthplace of Henry VIII, finishing school for the Royal Navy when Britannia really did rule the waves, and home to time itself. This walk—short in distance but including a sharp uphill climb to the Observatory—takes in some of London's finest architecture and an iconic panorama. When you're visiting a borough famed for maritime heritage, there's only one proper way to arrive: by boat. START: Thames Clipper to Greenwich Pier (or DLR to Cutty Sark).

Old Royal Naval College.

1 ★★ kids Cutty Sark. You can walk in, on, and even under "the fastest ship in the world," a majestic 3-masted clipper launched in 1869 to import tea from China (and which later switched to carrying Merino wool from Australia). Over 52 years of service it set several records and could reach top speeds of around 20 miles per hour. Despite a catastrophic 2007 fire, about 90% of the structure you see is original. Feeling brave? Upgrade your admission ticket to climb the rigging and shuffle out on one of the topsail yards. ⏱ *45 min.* ☎ *020/8312-6608. rmg.*

co.uk/cutty-sark. £18 adults, £9 children 4–15; £27/£13.50 combo ticket with Royal Observatory, **7**; £52 adults, £43 children 10–15 including rig climb. Daily 10am–6pm.

2 ★★★ Old Royal Naval College. An architectural masterpiece, these buildings were originally the Greenwich Hospital, a home for retired Royal Navy seamen. Such was its prestige that Wren, Hawksmoor, and Sir John Vanbrugh all worked on the project from the 1690s onward. Converted to a Royal Navy training college in 1873, it's now largely used by the University of Greenwich—and film crews from all over the world. ⏱ *20 min.* ☎ *020/8269-4799. ornc.org. Free admission.*

3 ★★★ Painted Hall. No, you haven't been teleported to Renaissance Florence. This vast hall was intended to be the hospital dining room but was quickly deemed far too ornate for that. Sir James Thornhill took 19 years to cover 40,000 sq.-ft. of wall and ceiling in a baroque buffet of allegory, mythology, and grandiloquent propaganda—with Protestant monarchs William and Mary at the center of it all. An admission ticket also includes a guided tour covering history, architecture, or notable film locations (at least one of them runs each day). ⏱ *40 min.* ☎ *020/8269-4799. ornc.org. £15 adults, free children 16 & under. Daily 10am–5pm.*

National Maritime Museum.

4 ★ kids **Greenwich Market** has operated in one form or another since 1737. Its current incarnation is an on-trend jumble of maker stalls, vintage vinyl, crafts, curios, and street food covering everything from vegan to Venezuelan. *College Approach.* ☎ 020/8269-5096. greenwich market.london. £.

5 ★★★ kids **National Maritime Museum.** This interactive, child-friendly collection is also a world-class repository of seafaring history, artefacts, and art. Undoubted star painting is Turner's *Battle of Trafalgar, 1805,* which gets a room to itself. It celebrates a famous victory at sea against a combined French and Spanish fleet, during which around 8,000 seamen were wounded or killed, including the English commander Admiral Lord Nelson (also immortalized in Trafalgar Square; p 21, **5**). More somber galleries examine the complex legacy of the East

India Company, a conglomerate of English merchants who grew rich and powerful on tea and textile trading from the 1600s and who eventually became the de facto government of South Asia. In a checkered history of warmongering, piracy, coercion, colonial profiteering, and worse, the Company's involvement in the Opium Wars with China (1839–42) stand out: "A war more unjust in its origins, a war more calculated… to cover this country with disgrace, I do not know," in the words of William Gladstone, who became Britain's prime minister on four separate occasions. ⏱ 1¼ hr. ☎ 020/8312-6608. rmg.co.uk/national-maritime-museum. Free admission. Daily 10am–5pm.

6 ★★ **Queen's House.** This icon of Jacobean architecture, Greenwich's oldest major building, was created by Inigo Jones for Anne of Denmark, wife of King James I. Heavily influenced by the architectural theories of Italian Andrea Palladio, whose ideas also shaped the design of capitol buildings across America, Jones made this England's first Classical building. Immaculate in preservation and elegant in proportion, its highlights include the **Great Hall**—a perfect cube—and the **Tulip** spiral staircase. In later years the building housed royal servants and provided studio space for painters including the Van der Veldes, whose nautical works remain on display. ○ *45 min.* ☎ *020/8312-6608. rmg.co.uk/ queens-house. Free admission. Daily 10am–5pm.*

⑦ ★★ Royal Observatory, Greenwich. This complex dedicated to the study of the heavens was HQ of British astronomy for almost 300 years. It's still the spot from where the world sets its clock: Greenwich Mean Time. Rather than wait in line for a pointless selfie straddling the Meridian Line, with a foot in each hemisphere, instead take in the fascinating astronomical exhibits. These include a room dedicated to the problem of measuring longitude, a solution so important to maritime navigation that the government of 1714 offered a prize equivalent to £1.4m ($1.8m) in today's money. ○ *1 hr.* ☎ *020/8312-6608. rmg.co.uk/royal-observatory. £18 adults, £9 children 4–15; £27/£13.50 combo ticket with Cutty Sark, ❶. Daily 10am–6pm.*

❽ ★★★ kids Greenwich Park. Right in front of the statue of General James Wolfe, killed defeating the French at the Battle of Quebec (1779), is one of the best views of London—maybe my favorite. The towers of Canary Wharf and Docklands loom directly above the Old Royal Naval College (❷). To the west stand the Shard and City skyscrapers; to the east, the UFO-like Millennium Dome, now a concert venue (p 134). Descend (slightly) and tack a little right to **One Tree Hill,** for a similar panorama and a view back to the Observatory. When snow falls, this park becomes an impromptu tobogganing hill. ○ *20 min. royalparks.org.uk/parks/ greenwich-park. Daily 6am–9:30pm.*

Entrance to the Queen's House.

64

Mayfair

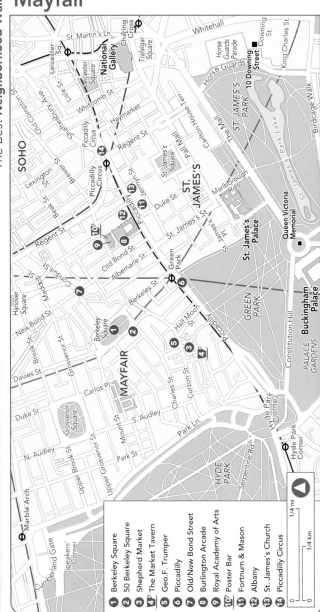

1 Berkeley Square
2 50 Berkeley Square
3 Shepherd Market
4 The Market Tavern
5 Geo. F. Trumper
6 Piccadilly
7 Old/New Bond Street
8 Burlington Arcade
9 Royal Academy of Arts
10 Poster Bar
11 Fortnum & Mason
12 Albany
13 St. James's Church
14 Piccadilly Circus

For more than 3 centuries, Mayfair has been an enclave of the aristocracy, who lived in grand style inside elegant mansions run by armies of servants. Enough of these urban palaces survive to make a walk around this exclusive neighborhood a fascinating glimpse into how London's rich lived—and in part, still live. This half-day walk focuses on the southern part of Mayfair. START: **Tube to Green Park.**

Berkeley Square Park.

❶ ★★ Berkeley Square. Laid out in the 18th century on part of Lord Berkeley's London estate, this grand square has long been one of the capital's most-sought-after addresses. Notables who have called the square home include prime ministers Winston Churchill (who lived at no. 48 as a boy) and George Canning (who resided briefly at no. 50; see ❷). The modern east side is now undistinguished office buildings. The plane trees surrounding the square were planted in 1789 and are among the oldest in the city.

❷ 50 Berkeley Square. This Georgian-style building was famed as the "most haunted house in London" in the 19th century, when sightings of a bewigged man and sounds of an unearthly nature kept the house untenanted. Although

strange happenings have been reported here in recent years, the worst of it seems to have taken place in Victorian days, when an evil presence so terrified a visitor that he threw himself out the window and was impaled on the railings below.

❸ ★★ Shepherd Market. In the mid-18th century, the riotous May Fair (which gave the neighborhood its name) was banned and the land was redeveloped by architect Edward Shepherd. The result was much what you see now: charming yet humble buildings from the days when these few streets were the hub of the servant classes in Mayfair. Today it's lined with traditional pubs, wine bars, and restaurants serving various cuisines: French, Italian, Lebanese, Polish, and more.

The famed façade of the Ritz Hotel.

A favorite with the after-work crowd, **4** ★ **The Market Tavern** is a homey, wood-floored pub with a good selection of small plates for a light lunch, such as soft-shell crab with pickled ginger mayo. *7 Shepherd St.* ☎ *020/7491-0910. themarkettavernmayfair.co.uk. £–££.*

5 ★ **Geo. F. Trumper.** This English institution opened in 1875, and still offers traditional wet shaves with straight razors and hot towels, mustache trimming, and—in a concession to the more fluid 2020s—manicures. Even if you don't need a shave or toiletries, do have a look around the wonderful shop. *9 Curzon St.* ☎ *020/7499-1850. trumpers.com. Closed Sun.*

6 ★★ **Piccadilly.** The name Piccadilly is said to have come from the word *picadil*, a stiff collar manufactured by an early-17th-century tailor who bought a parcel of land here on which he built a grand home. Lest the upstart forget his humble beginnings, it was sneeringly referred to as "Piccadilly Hall." In the 18th and 19th centuries, many great mansions were built along the street facing Green Park. Head east on Piccadilly so you can admire the elaborate gates surrounding Green Park and the carved classical-style heads on the Parisian-inspired facade of the Ritz Hotel.

7 ★★ **Old & New Bond Street.** Perhaps the smartest shopping street in London, lined end to end with boutiques from some of the biggest names in fashion and jewelry (Prada, Tiffany, Louis Vuitton, Bulgari) and not a price tag in sight (if you have to ask…). The point where Old Bond Street meets New is marked with a statue of President Franklin D. Roosevelt and prime minister Churchill chatting on a bench.

8 ★★ **Burlington Arcade.** Opened in 1819, this is a very *haute* mall of around 40 elegant shops with curved glass windows and mahogany fronts, selling jewelry, upmarket

Burlington Arcade opened in 1819.

clothing, shoes, accessories, and art. Top-hatted, frock-coated guards are employed to make sure nobody does anything as uncouth as running, whistling, or singing inside the arcade. *51 Piccadilly. No phone. burlingtonarcade.com.*

⑨ ★★ Royal Academy of Arts. Burlington House, built in the 1660s, was a magnificent estate later purchased by the government (in 1854) to house England's oldest arts society. The Royal Academy has staged a "Summer Exhibition" for more than 200 years now, making this the home of the world's longest-running open-submission competition. These days, however, its major draws are blockbuster temporary shows, often showcasing the biggest names from art's past or present. They also offer free access to some of the permanent collection on rotation: Visit the **Collection Gallery** for a Joshua Reynolds portrait or Michelangelo sculpture. ⏱ *45 min. Burlington House, Piccadilly.* ☎ *020/7300-8090. royalacademy.org.uk. Tues–Sun 10am–6pm (Fri closes 9pm). Admission prices vary by exhibition (typically £15–£28); free admission to Collection Gallery.*

Shopping in Fortnum & Mason.

The RA's 10 ★ **Poster Bar**, overseen by Spanish culinary Don, José Pizarro, serves classic tapas and tostadas, with Spanish wine to wash it down. *Burlington Gardens Entrance. No phone. £.££.*

⑪ ★★★ **Fortnum & Mason.** A famous partnership began in 1705 when shop owner Hugh Mason let a room to William Fortnum, a footman for Queen Anne at the Palace of St. James. The enterprising Fortnum "recycled" candle ends from the palace (the queen required fresh candles nightly) and sold them to Mason. From this humble beginning, Fortnum & Mason grew to rule Britannia (or at least Piccadilly) with one of the earliest globally recognized brand names. Its hampers are legendary. For a refined afternoon tea (£78/person), try the **Diamond Jubilee Tea Salon** on the fourth floor. *181 Piccadilly. fortnumandmason.com. See also p 93.*

⑫ **Albany.** Built in the 1770s by architect William Chambers for Lord Melbourne, this grand Georgian building was turned into a residence for gentlemen in 1802. Since then, many poets (Lord Byron), authors (Graham Greene), playwrights (J. B. Priestley), prime ministers, and even fictional characters of Dickens, Wilde, and Conan Doyle have called this exclusive bachelor patch home. Marking a revolutionary leap into the modern world, women are now allowed to live here (but no children under 14).

Traditions are maintained via the rigid use of terminology: Dwellings are not flats or apartments but "sets," and the building is strictly "Albany," never "The Albany." *Albany Yard, Piccadilly.*

⑬ ★ **St. James's Church.** This unprepossessing redbrick church is one of Christopher Wren's simplest, said by Charles Dickens to be "not one of the master's happiest efforts." The poet William Blake was baptized here, as was William Pitt, the first earl of Chatham, who became England's youngest prime minister at the age of 24. You are welcome to enter and sit in quiet or enjoy a free lunchtime recital (donations requested). There's plenty more music, too, including candlelight concerts (usually Sat) and Sunday soul and gospel sessions. ① *15 min. 197 Piccadilly.* ☎ *020/ 7734-4511. sjp.org.uk. Recitals usually Wed & Fri 1pm; candlelight concerts £22–£38.*

⑭ ★ **Piccadilly Circus.** London's slightly underwhelming answer to New York's Times Square was the first place in the city to have electrical signage, and its glaring neon (and now digital) billboards have graced a million postcards and movies. The word "circus" refers to a circular juncture at an intersection of streets. The plaza was built in 1819 to connect two of London's major shopping boulevards, Regent Street and Piccadilly. The statue popularly known as Eros (for trivia fans: It's actually Anteros, the Greek god of requited love) on the central island is a favorite meeting place.

69

The East by Overground

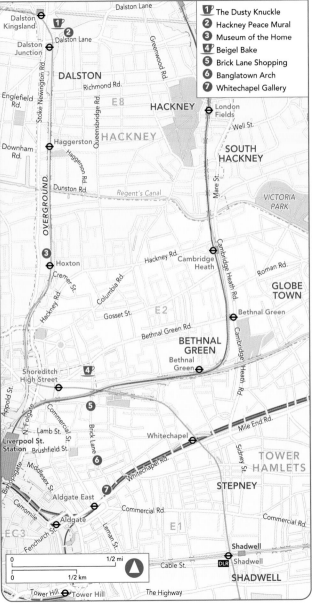

1 The Dusty Knuckle
2 Hackney Peace Mural
3 Museum of the Home
4 Beigel Bake
5 Brick Lane Shopping
6 Banglatown Arch
7 Whitechapel Gallery

East London bore the brunt of World War II bombing, so historic buildings are thinner on the ground. Easily reached and navigated by air-conditioned Overground train (an extension of the Tube), it's become a food, shopping, and nightlife wonderland. But much more, too: Radical politics and sweeping social change have molded a younger, livelier London than you'll encounter "Up West." START: **Overground to Dalston Junction or Dalston Kingsland.**

What if I told you that ☕ ★★★ **kids The Dusty Knuckle** was London's best bakery? I've not eaten in every single one, of course, but I don't know a better start to the day than a coffee and one of their enormous sticky buns. *Abbot St. Car Park. No phone. thedustyknuckle. com. £.*

❷ ★★ **Hackney Peace Mural.** A vibrant reminder of the neighborhood's anti-establishment history—and love of a street party—this giant 1980s mural was commissioned to show Hackney's commitment to multiracial harmony and nuclear disarmament. *17 Dalston Ln. Overground: Dalston Junction.*

❸ ★★ **kids Museum of the Home.** Over two floors, these converted almshouses track the development of domestic spaces in London through the ages. The ground floor divides into rooms tricked out as middle-class residences from 1630 onward—all original, no replicas. Downstairs, multimedia exhibits explore how domestic aesthetics and the meaning of "home" have evolved. Out back "Gardens Through Time" provides green-fingered insights. ⏱ 1¼ hr. *136 Kingsland Rd. No phone. museumofthehome.org.uk. Free admission; £5 guided tour (Sat 2pm). Tues–Sun 10am–4pm. Overground: Hoxton.*

1970s room at Museum of the Home.

Bustling Brick Lane.

Poor Jewish immigrants settled London's East End in the late-19th century. A £5 loaded salt beef bagel with pickles and fiery mustard from **4** ★★ kids **Beigel Bake Brick Lane Bakery** is a tasty reminder of one enduring legacy.

When you see the (fast-moving) line, you're in the right place. *159 Brick Ln.* ☎ *020/7729-0616. brick-lanebeigel.co.uk. Open 24 hr. £.*

5 ★★★ **Vintage Shopping along Brick Lane.** Some of London's best thrift stores open every day of the week. On weekends, the buzzing **Upmarket** (p 95) fills the streets. See "Shopping," p 83.

6 ★ **Banglatown Arch & Mural.** Postwar Bengali immigration to this ever-changing neighborhood is celebrated with this stylized Islamic-Indian arch and a mural by artist Mohammed Ali—unveiled in 2022 to mark 50 years of Bangladeshi independence from Britain. *Corner of Brick Ln. & Hopetown St.*

7 ★★ **Whitechapel Gallery.** Founded in 1901, this museum has a proud history of activist art and community education. In 1938, Picasso's "Guernica" was exhibited here in protest against Fascism and the Spanish Civil War. The building itself is a rare (for London) example of Art Nouveau.

Banglatown Arch and Mural.

Hampstead

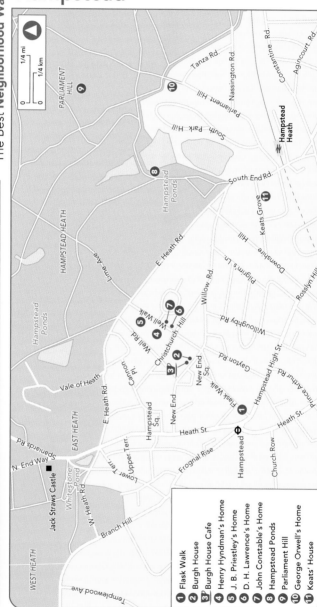

1/4 mi
1/4 km

PARLIAMENT HILL

Tanza Rd.

Constantine Rd.

Agincourt Rd.

Nassington Rd.

Parliament Hill

South Park Hill

Hampstead Heath

HAMPSTEAD HEATH

South End Rd.

Hampstead Ponds

Keats Grove

Limeau Ave.

E. Heath Rd.

Downshire Hill

Rosslyn Hill

Pilgrim's Ln.

Hampstead Ponds

Willow Rd.

Willoughby Rd.

Vale of Heath

Christchurch Hill

Cannon Pl.

Well Rd.

Well Walk

Gayton Rd.

Hampstead High St.

E. Heath Rd.

New End

New End Sq.

Flask Walk

Prince Arthur Rd.

Hampstead Sq.

Heath St.

Heath St.

Spaniards Rd.

Lower Terr.

Upper Terr.

Frognal Rise

Hampstead

Church Row

N. End Way

EAST HEATH

Jack Straws Castle

Whitestone Pond

W. Heath Rd.

Branch Hill

WEST HEATH

Templewood Ave.

❶ Flask Walk
❷ Burgh House
❸ Burgh House Cafe
❹ Henry Hyndman's Home
❺ J. B. Priestley's Home
❻ D. H. Lawrence's Home
❼ John Constable's Home
❽ Hampstead Ponds
❾ Parliament Hill
❿ George Orwell's Home
⓫ Keats' House

Hampstead first became popular during the Great Plague of 1665, when well-to-do Londoners escaped here from the contagion of their neighborhoods. Today, it is still a genteel refuge, known for historic buildings, a rich artistic and literary legacy, and proximity to the Heath, 324 hectares (800 acres) of loosely managed wilderness and far-reaching views across the city. START: **Tube to Hampstead.**

1 ★★ Flask Walk. Now a narrow alley of chichi shops leading to a street of expensive homes, Flask Walk was the site of early–18th-century fairs and of year-round establishments for drinking and gambling—all built to entertain the crush of Londoners escaping fetid city streets for Hampstead's fresh air. The street was named after a now-defunct tavern that bottled the village's pure water and hawked it around London.

2 ★★ Burgh House. Built in 1704, this restored Queen Anne structure, former home of spa physician Dr. William Gibbon, is now a museum of Hampstead history. It also stages rotating art exhibitions, talks, classes and workshops, and evening classical music recitals. ⏱ *30 min. New End Sq.* ☎ *020/ 7431-0144. burghhouse.org.uk. Free admission. Wed–Fri & Sun 10am– 4pm. Tube: Hampstead.*

In the Burgh House basement, the **3 ★★ Burgh House Café** serves great home-made cakes, as well as all-day brunch, toasties, and hearty salads. The garden is a charming spot for a slow lunch on a sunny afternoon. *New End Sq.* ☎ *020/7794-3943. Closed Mon– Tues. £–££.*

4 ★ Henry Hyndman's Home. A journalist, politician, and public speaker, Hyndman (1842–1921) founded the Social Democratic Federation, England's first socialist party, in 1881. He lived in this house until his death in 1921. *13 Well Walk.*

5 J. B. Priestley's Home. One of England's most prolific men of letters, Priestley (1894–1984) was an essayist, playwright, biographer, historian, and social commentator who refused a knighthood and peerage. He lived in this Queen Anne–style house from 1928 to 1932. *27 Well Walk.*

6 D. H. Lawrence's Home. During World War I, Lawrence (1885–1930) hoboed around Hampstead, including here, after being kicked out of Cornwall when his wife was unjustly accused of being a German spy. He left in 1919 for Italy, where he wrote his most famous novel, *Lady Chatterley's Lover,* in 1928. The book was banned in Britain on charges of indecency and wasn't published here uncensored until 1960. *32 Well Walk.*

7 John Constable's Home. The quintessential English landscape and portrait painter resided here from 1827 until his death in 1837. It was in his many studies of nearby Hampstead Heath that Constable mastered the depiction of weather in landscapes, tirelessly painting the same scene in different climatic conditions. The house is marked with a blue plaque. *40 Well Walk.*

8 ★★ Hampstead Ponds. Hampstead has three lovely woodland swimming ponds—former res-

Swimming in the mixed pond at Hampstead.

ervoirs dug in the mid-19th century—where you can take a refreshing open-air dip (the water is often cold). There's a men's pond, a ladies' pond, and a mixed pond, which gets particularly busy in summer. *Hampstead Heath.* ☎ *020/ 7332-3779. cityoflondon.gov.uk/ things-to-do. £4.50 adults, £2.70 seniors & children 15 & under. Daily 7am–dusk (exact times vary); mixed pond closed in winter. Overground: Hampstead Heath.*

⑨ ★★★ Parliament Hill. According to legend, the men behind the 1605 Gunpowder Plot planned to watch Parliament blown sky-high from this elevated vantage point. Fittingly, it's now one of the best places to watch the fireworks staged every November 5 to commemorate the foiling of the plot. Daytime views are no less dramatic; a map on the site identifies the buildings spread out before you. *Inside Hampstead Heath.*

⑩ ★ George Orwell's Home. The author of *Animal Farm, 1984,* and *Down and Out in Paris and London* wrote the satirical *Keep the Aspidistra Flying* in a back room on an upper floor of this house. He lived here for only 6 months in 1935 while working part-time at Booklover's Corner, a small bookstore on South End Green (now a chain bakery). *77 Parliament Hill.*

Parliament Hill, overlooking London.

The Loos of London

London once had plenty of public lavatories. Time was when nearly every high street boasted its own well-maintained convenience, but now they're few and far between. The old-fashioned tiled underground facilities have almost completely disappeared (they're expensive to maintain) while the free-standing kiosks (nicknamed "super loos") are increasingly thin on the ground. If you get caught short, however, many major train stations have public lavatories, typically requiring a 50p or £1 coin. Other options include museums and galleries, most of which are free and have modern, clean facilities, or toilets in many public parks. Department stores are another good bet, as are fast-food restaurants. Come the evening, however, your best option may be to nip into the nearest pub, where the polite protocol is to first buy a little something to become a customer. (But if the bar is crowded and you're desperate, scan quickly for the stairs: Central London pub toilets are often in the basement.)

⓫ ★★ **Keats' House.** The Romantic poet John Keats lived just 2 years at this Regency house but found enough time to write some of his most famous works, including *Ode to a Nightingale*, and to fall in love with next-door neighbor Fanny Brawne, his eventual fiancée (and the muse behind much of his best poetry). In 1820, he traveled to Italy, where he died of tuberculosis a few months later. The house is now a museum dedicated to the poet's life and displays original manuscripts and portraits. ⏱ *1 hr. 10 Keats Grove.* ☎ *020/7332-3868. cityoflondon.gov.uk/keats. £8.50 adults, free children 18 & under. Wed–Fri & Sun 11am–1pm & 2–5pm. Overground: Hampstead Heath.*

Shops in Hampstead Heath.

The City & Spitalfields

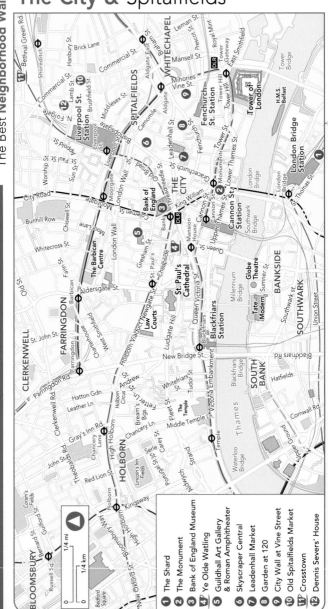

1 The Shard
2 The Monument
3 Bank of England Museum
4 Ye Olde Watling
5 Guildhall Art Gallery & Roman Amphitheater
6 Skyscraper Central
7 Leadenhall Market
8 Garden at 120
9 City Wall at Vine Street
10 Old Spitalfields Market
11 Crosstown
12 Dennis Severs' House

Roam where it all began: in the Square Mile, aka "the City." The site of the first London settlement founded by the Romans 2,000 years ago continues to thrive as a major global financial center. Astonishingly, much land here is still owned by the City Livery Companies, trades guilds that ran almost everything in medieval times. You will spot gardens, buildings, or streets that reference Drapers (cloth merchants), Mercers (butchers), Carpenters, and many others. Onward from here begins the East End, once the impoverished haunt of Jack the Ripper but now where arts, shopping, and nightlife bloom. START: **Tube to London Bridge.**

The Monument.

① ★★ kids **The Shard.** This great, pointy, 72-story glass skyscraper is Western Europe's tallest building. Standing 310m (1,017-ft.) high, it towers over London Bridge Station like a shiny pyramid. Its observation decks have London's loftiest view, offering unprecedented (and giddying) panoramas over the City of London, which lies across the River Thames. Historically speaking, you're not (yet) in London, but in Southwark. ⏱ *1 hr. Joiner St.* ☎ *0344/499-7222. theviewfromtheshard.com. £32 adults, £25 children 5–15, £80 family. Thurs–Sat 10am–10pm, Sun–Wed 11am–7pm. Tube: London Bridge.*

② ★★★ kids **The Monument.** Sir Christopher Wren designed this 62m-high (202-ft.) Doric stone column—topped with a gilded fiery urn—to commemorate the Great Fire of 1666. That tragic disaster started on September 2, inside the house of a baker on Pudding Lane (the height of the tower corresponds to the distance from its base to the fire's starting point). A stiff wind ignited the old timber-and-thatch houses of the City; more than 13,000 homes and 87 churches were reduced to smoldering ash. It's 311 steps to the top, from where the views are still among the best in the City, despite the fact that surrounding buildings are somewhat taller than in Wren's day. ⏱ *30 min. Monument St. No phone. the monument.info. £6 adults, £4.50 seniors, £3 children 5–15. Daily 9:30am–1pm & 2–5:30pm. Tube: Monument.*

③ ★★ **Bank of England Museum.** Take a close-up look at the glue that holds the Square Mile together: money. The world's second-oldest central bank was originally founded, in 1694, as a private joint-stock company. Its story, told

The Gherkin skyscraper.

admirably here, mirrors the history of modern banking, and includes frank exhibits on the Bank's role in funding transatlantic slave traders in the 1700s. One "lighter" highlight is a gold bar weighing 400 troy ounces. It can be touched but—no matter how you wiggle your hand inside the Perspex box—not removed. ⏱ *1 hr. Bartholomew Lane.* ☎ *020/3461-5545. bankofengland.co.uk/museum. Free admission. Mon–Fri 10am–5pm (3rd Thurs of month until 7:30pm). Tube: Bank.*

Just south of St. Mary-le-Bow, the "Cockney Church," is London's oldest road, Watling Street, which 1,900 years ago linked the capital with the coast. Here you'll find the aged—if not quite so venerable— **4** ★ **Ye Olde Watling.** Built in the 17th century out of ships' timbers, it serves decent pub grub and a range of ales. *29 Watling St.* ☎ *020/7248-8935. nicholsonspubs.co.uk. Closed Sun. £–££.*

5 ★★ **Guildhall Art Gallery & Roman Amphitheatre.** A 1990s extension of the City's medieval and much-restored Guildhall holds an art gallery showcasing a rotating selection from its 4,000-plus London-related works. The collection is strong on Victorian-era painters. In the basement are the remains of London's Roman amphitheater. ⏱ *1 hr. Guildhall Yard, off Gresham St.* ☎ *020/7332-3700. cityoflondon.gov.uk/guildhallgalleries. Free admission. Daily 10:30am–4pm. Tube: Bank or Moorgate.*

6 ★ **kids Skyscraper Central.** Just off Bishopsgate, the small square of Great St. Helen's neatly encapsulates how the City's skyline has changed over the centuries. At its center is the almost fragile-looking, 13th-century **St. Helen's Church,** while on all sides loom skyscrapers. From the church courtyard, you can see to the west **Tower 42,** formerly the City's tallest building, and to the east the **Gherkin** (more formally, 30 St. Mary Axe). To the south, new steel-and-glass giants keep rising at a rapid rate, including buildings imaginatively nicknamed the **Cheesegrater** (122 Leadenhall St.); the **Walkie-Talkie** (20 Fenchurch St.; home to the Sky Garden, p 131); the **Scalpel** (50 Lime St.); and more prosaically, directly overhead, **Twentytwo** (22 Bishopsgate), at 278m (912 ft.) the tallest building in the Square Mile. *Gt. St. Helen's.*

7 ★★ Leadenhall Market. A Victorian gem, this photogenic covered market was built in the 1880s. The site is much, much older: The market gained its charter in 1321, and the Roman Forum is right below your feet. Leadenhall's watering holes are popular with City workers winding down at the end of the day. ⏱ *10 min. Tube: Bank.*

8 ★★★ kids The Garden at 120. Fifteen stories high, this rooftop garden with 360-degree panorama is nestled amid London's tallest towers—the Walkie-Talkie feels close enough to touch—with knockout views south to the Shard and Tower Bridge. Way to the south, that's not the Eiffel Tower, but the Crystal Palace TV transmitter, built on the site of Britain's first color TV broadcasts. The Garden is completely free to visit—just turn up and ride up. ⏱ *25 min. 120 Fenchurch St. No phone. thegarden at120.com. Free admission. Mon–Fri 10am–6:30pm (Apr–Sept until 9pm), Sat–Sun 10am–5pm. Closed national holidays. Tube: Aldgate or Tower Hill.*

9 ★★ City Wall at Vine Street. One unearthed slice of London's original 2-mile defensive ring—almost 2,000 years old—manages to encapsulate the story of the city itself. These hunks of limestone have kept Saxon invaders at bay, propped up glassmakers' and gunmakers' workshops, and served as sturdy foundations for warehouses and now a student accommodation block. ⏱ *30 min. 12 Jewry St. No phone. citywallvinestreet.org. Free admission (prebooking essential). Daily 9am–6pm. Tube: Aldgate.*

10 ★ kids Old Spitalfields Market. The latest, now somewhat sanitized version of the gnarly old market preserves some Victorian atmosphere amid modern redevelopment: There's street food, eclectic clothes and crafts, and a few chains. Best of all: It's covered, an ideal rain break. ⏱ *30 min. ☎ 020/7377-1496. spitalfields.co.uk. Tube: Liverpool St.*

At **11 ★ kids Crosstown** chow down on creatively flavored donuts to die for, regular and vegan. *157 Brick Lane. ☎ 020/7729-3417. crosstown.co.uk. £.*

12 ★★ Dennis Severs' House. From 1979 until his death in 1999, American expat Dennis Severs not only restored his Spitalfields townhouse to its early–18th-century prime but also created a fictional backstory for it, as a refuge for the Jervises, a family of Huguenots who fled persecution in France. The rooms have been arranged as if just vacated by these occupants, and the result is fascinatingly odd. The house is at its most atmospheric during candlelit "Silent Night" visits on Friday evenings. ⏱ *45 min. 18 Folgate St. No phone. dennissevershouse.co.uk. £15 adults, £10 seniors & students; £20 "Silent Nights." Thurs–Sun hours vary (see website). Tube: Liverpool St.*

Dennis Severs' House.

Whitehall

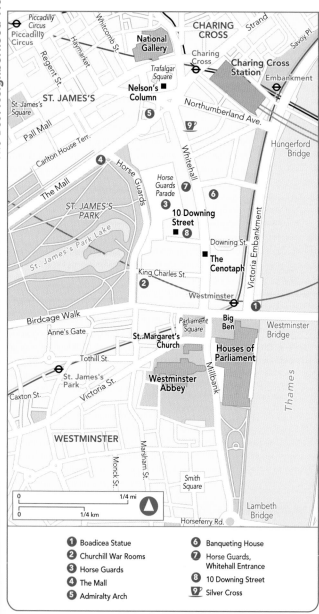

1 Boadicea Statue
2 Churchill War Rooms
3 Horse Guards
4 The Mall
5 Admiralty Arch

6 Banqueting House
7 Horse Guards,
   Whitehall Entrance
8 10 Downing Street
9 Silver Cross

Once the site of the vast Palace of Whitehall—London's chief royal residence from 1530 to 1698—this area is now a neighborhood of government buildings whose architecture confers a certain grandeur to the dull business of bureaucracy. This half-day walk is best in the morning; time things to arrive at Horse Guards Parade to see the Changing of the Life Guard. START: **Tube to Westminster.**

❶ **Boadicea Statue.** A tall and ferocious queen of the Iceni tribe of East Anglia, Boadicea waged battle against Britain's 1st-century Roman invaders, nailing captured soldiers to trees and flaying them alive. In A.D. 61, her forces temporarily took Londinium before they were thoroughly defeated by the Roman army. The queen (whose name means victorious) became a heroic figure of Victorian England. This statue by Thomas Thornycroft was erected in 1902. *Bridge St. & Victoria Embankment.*

❷ ★★★ kids **Churchill War Rooms.** British Prime Minister Winston Churchill directed World War II from this underground shelter as German bombs rained down on London. The basements of these Civil Service buildings were redesigned in the war to house a hospital, a cafeteria, sleeping quarters, and even a shooting range. After the war, the area was locked and left untouched until 1984, when Churchill's quarters were turned into a museum; all the items you see are the genuine article. Interactive displays also tell the story of Churchill's life and career. ⏱ 1¼ hr. *Clive Steps, King Charles St.* ☎ 020/ 7091-3067. iwm.org.uk. £27 adults, £24.50 seniors, £14 children 5–15. Daily 9:30am–6pm.

❸ ★★ kids **Horse Guards.** This grand 18th-century building is the headquarters of the Household Cavalry Mounted Regiment, chief bodyguards of the monarch. At a small on-site museum, you can see members tending to their horses in the adjacent stables, through a glass partition. The large parade ground out front is the site for the annual **Trooping the Colour** ceremony. Every day at 11am (10am on Sun) there's a **Changing of the Life Guard** ceremony, much mellower (and less crowded) than you'll find outside Buckingham Palace (p 37, ❷). ⏱ 45 min. *Horse Guards. Household Cavalry Museum:* ☎ 020/ 7930-3070. householdcavalry.co.uk/ museum. £10 adults, £8 children 5–16, £27.50 family (2+3). Daily 10am–5pm (Apr–Oct until 6pm).

❹ ★★ **The Mall.** This red-gravel thoroughfare—running northeast from Buckingham Palace (p 37, ❷) to Trafalgar Square (p 21, ❺)—was created in 1660 as a venue for St. James's gallants to play the popular game of *paille maille* (a precursor to croquet). In the early 18th century, it was a fashionable promenade for the beau monde, and in 1903 was redesigned as a processional route for royal occasions. When foreign heads of state visit the monarch, the Mall is decked out in the Union Jack and the flag of the visitor's country. *Between Buckingham Palace & Admiralty Arch.*

❺ ★★ **Admiralty Arch.** Built in 1910, this quintuple-arched building looks southwest to the grand statue of Queen Victoria in front of Buckingham Palace. The central gates are for ceremonial use, opening only to let a royal procession pass. Adorable little ships sitting atop nearby street lamps are a nod to the Old Admiralty Offices that inhabited the arch. Its lease now sold by the government, the arch will become a Waldorf Astoria hotel, opening in 2025.

❻ ★★★ Banqueting House. All that remains of Whitehall Palace is this grand hall, completed in 1621 by Inigo Jones. The city's first Renaissance-style construction was inspired by the Italian architecture of Palladio but is best known for a glorious Rubens-painted ceiling—commissioned by Charles I (1600–49), who used the building for elaborate parties called "masques" and for greeting foreign delegations (not actually for banqueting). The allegorical painting, equating the Stuart kings with the gods, may have gone to Charles's head: His stubborn belief in the divine right of kings led directly to the English Civil Wars and ultimately his execution for treason, right outside the hall. *Whitehall.* ⏱ *1 hr.* ☎ *0333/ 320-6000. hrp.org.uk/banqueting-house. £12.50 adults (guided tour). Dates vary; see website.*

❼ Horse Guards, Whitehall Entrance. Just across from the Banqueting House is another entrance to Horse Guards Parade, guarded by mounted soldiers in ceremonial garb who provide good photo opportunities for visitors. Through the gates an arched tunnel frames a beautiful view of St. James's Park.

❽ 10 Downing St. The home address of Britain's prime minister since 1732 is set in a quiet cul-de-sac blocked off by iron gates for security reasons. There's not much to see now except a lot of police giving you the evil eye, though there is a *frisson* of excitement to be had by standing near so much power.

Of many pubs along Whitehall, my favorite is the **❾ ★ Silver Cross,** which, despite some faux ye olde England decor, is genuinely old (it was granted a brothel license in 1674). It offers filling fish and chips, lots of seating, and its own ghost—a young girl in Tudor dress. *33 Whitehall.* ☎ *020/7930-8350. £–££.* ●

10 Downing St.

Shopping Best Bets

Best **Time to Shop**
During the July/August and December/January citywide sales

Best for **Last Season's Designer Dresses at Big Discounts**
★★ Pandora Dress Agency, *16–22 Cheval Pl. (p 91)*

Best for the **London Look**
★★ John Smedley, *24 Brook St. (p 91)*; or ★★ Fred Perry, *12 Newburgh St. (p 90)*

Best for **Vintage Jewelry**
★★★ Hirst Collection, *59 Pembridge Rd. (p 94)*

Best for a **Sugar Rush**
★★ Artisan du Chocolat, *89 Lower Sloane St. (p 92)*

Most Famous **Toy Store**
★ Hamleys, *189–196 Regent St. (p 96)*

Best Place to **Score Amazing Items from Someone Else's Attic**
★★★ Alfies Antique Market, *13–25 Church St. (p 88)*; or ★★★ Grays Antique Market, *58 Davies St. (p 88)*

Best for **Comics & Graphic Novels**
★★ Gosh! Comics, *1 Berwick St. (p 90)*; or ★★★ Forbidden Planet, *179 Shaftesbury Ave. (p 96)*

Best Place to **Drop a Pin**
★★ Stanfords, *7 Mercer Walk (p 90)*

Best for **Hot-Date Lingerie**
★★★ Selfridges, *400 Oxford St. (p 92)*

Best for **Foodies**
★★★ Borough Market, *Southwark St. (p 93)*; ★★★ Neal's Yard Dairy, *8 Park St. (p 93)*; or ★★★ Ottolenghi, *63 Ledbury Rd. (p 93)*

Best for **Vintage Street Fashion**
★★★ Brick Lane Vintage Market, *85 Brick Ln. (p 90)*

Best **Weekend Markets**
★★★ Portobello Road Market, *Portobello Rd. (p 96)*; or ★★ Upmarket, *Brick Ln. (p 95)*

Best for **Everything Under One Roof**
★★★ Selfridges, *400 Oxford St. (p 92)*; or ★★★ Liberty, *Regent St. (p 95)*

Best **Museum Shop**
★★ Victoria & Albert Museum, *Cromwell Rd. (p 96)*

Best **Parfumerie**
★★★ Angela Flanders, *4 Artillery Passage (p 88)*

Best for **Scotch (No, Not the Tape)**
★★★ Milroy's of Soho, *3 Greek St. (p 93)*

Best **Affordable Areas to Just Wander and See What Grabs You**
Spitalfields/Brick Lane; Portobello Road (Notting Hill); or Seven Dials (Covent Garden)

Previous page: Vendor at Grays Antiques Market. Below: Head to Borough Market at lunchtime.

Chelsea & Knightsbridge Shopping

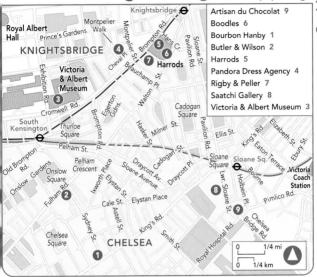

Artisan du Chocolat 9
Boodles 6
Bourbon Hanby 1
Butler & Wilson 2
Harrods 5
Pandora Dress Agency 4
Rigby & Peller 7
Saatchi Gallery 8
Victoria & Albert Museum 3

Nottingham Shopping

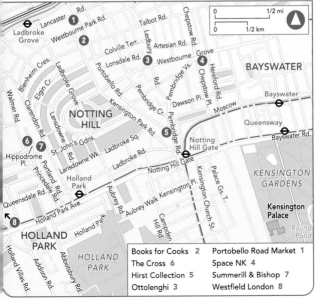

Books for Cooks 2
The Cross 6
Hirst Collection 5
Ottolenghi 3
Portobello Road Market 1
Space NK 4
Summerill & Bishop 7
Westfield London 8

The Best Shopping

Central & East London Shopping

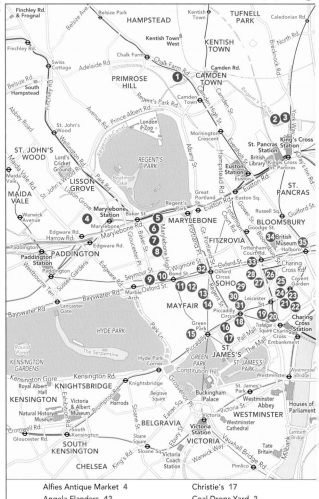

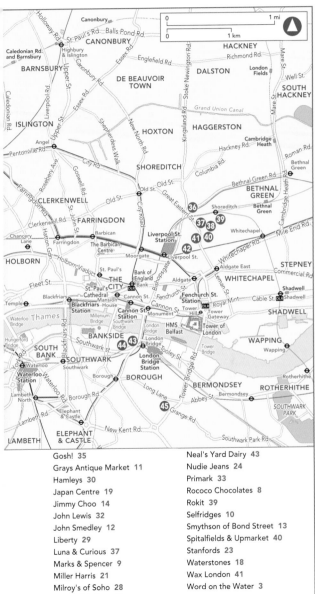

London Shopping A to Z

Anyone can attend an auction at Christie's.

Antiques & Auctions

★★★ Alfies Antique Market

MARYLEBONE   The city's largest indoor antique and flea market—four floors of secondhand knick-knacks, plus fabrics and dresses. Closed Sunday and Monday. *13–25 Church St.* ☎ *020/7723-6066. alfiesantiques.com. Tube: Marylebone. Map p 86.*

★★ Bermondsey (New Caledonian) Antiques Market

BERMONDSEY   Join the crush of dealers fighting over estate goods and antiques, sold here from 6am every Friday. Stalls are pretty much packed up and gone by lunchtime. *Corner of Bermondsey St. & Long Ln. bermondseyantiquemarket.co.uk. Tube: Bermondsey or Borough. Map p 86.*

★ Bourbon Hanby CHELSEA

A rather grand arcade of antiques stalls featuring upscale estate goods, jewelry, accessories, and even fine art. *151 Sydney St.* ☎ *020/7352-2106. bourbonhanby. com. Tube: Sloane Sq. Map p 85.*

★★ Christie's ST. JAMES'S

Don't be scared off by the serious treasures; this venerable auction house often has something unique for regular budgets, too. *8 King St.* ☎ *020/7839-9060. christies.com. Tube: Green Park. Map p 86.*

★★★ Grays Antique Market

MAYFAIR   Vendors across two neighboring sites sell everything from Art Deco paperweights and antique jewelry to Edwardian-era toys. *58 Davies St.* ☎ *020/7629-7034. graysantiques.com. Tube: Bond St. Map p 86.*

Beauty & Fragrances

★★★ Angela Flanders

SPITALFIELDS   This elegant boutique is well worth the effort it takes to find, in a passageway close to Old Spitalfields Market. Flanders' signature scents for men and women have a devoted clientele. *4 Artillery Passage.* ☎ *020/7247-7040. angelaflanders-perfumer.com. Tube: Liverpool St. Map p 86.*

★★ Geo. F. Trumper MAYFAIR

An essential shop for the well-groomed man, the woman who wants a great gift for her guy, or anyone interested in quality toiletries and shaving accessories. *9 Curzon St.* ☎ *020/7499-1850. trumpers. com. Tube: Green Park. Map p 86.*

Sales Tax

The U.K. levies a 20% Value Added Tax (VAT) on almost all non-essential purchases. Books, magazines, children's clothes and shoes, and a few other items are exempt from this sales tax. By law, VAT *must* be included in the retail price tag you see instore—there's no extra to pay at the checkout. There was a time when those who lived in North America (and anywhere outside Europe) could apply to have VAT refunded on large purchases. Alas, the "tax free shopping" bonus is no more. However, this remains a live political issue—a policy U-turn is not out of the question. For the latest, check **gov.uk/tax-on-shopping**.

★★ **Charlotte Tilbury** COVENT GARDEN Flagship store for the London luxury makeup brand loved by celebs and fashion photographers. *11–12 James St.* ☎ *020/3961-7160. charlottetilbury.com. Tube: Covent Garden. Map p 86.*

★★ **Miller Harris** COVENT GARDEN Trained in Grasse, France, Lyn Harris created a global brand of sexy and elegant scents of the finest quality, as well as beautifully packaged lotions and candles. *14 Monmouth St.* ☎ *020/3417-8070. millerharris.com. Tube: Covent Garden. Map p 86.*

★★ **Space NK** NOTTING HILL This upscale London chain sells many boutique lines of makeup, creams, fragrances, and decadent scented candles. *127–131 Westbourne Grove.* ☎ *020/7727-8063. spacenk.com. Tube: Notting Hill Gate or Bayswater. Map p 85.*

Books & Stationery
★★ **Books for Cooks** NOTTING HILL Recipe tomes for every conceivable cuisine or diet, plus a wider range of general culinary interest titles. *4 Blenheim Crescent.* ☎ *020/7221-1992. booksforcooks.com. Tube: Ladbroke Grove. Map p 85.*

★★★ **Daunt Books** MARYLEBONE The most atmospheric branch of a minichain still has its wonderful, century-old interior. It has an excellent travel section and the latest U.K. fiction, with a peaceful atmosphere for browsing. *83–84 Marylebone High St.*

Daunt Books on Marylebone High Street.

☎ 020/7224-2295. dauntbooks.
co.uk. Tube: Baker St. Map p 86.

★★ **Foyles** SOHO   The flagship
store of London's best-known independent bookseller has called this
street home since 1906. From aca-
demic to kids' books and London
guides, it's all here. *107 Charing
Cross Rd.* ☎ *020/7437-5660. foyles.
co.uk. Tube: Tottenham Court Rd.
Map p 86.*

★★ **Gosh! Comics** SOHO   Arthouse comics, special editions, and
mainstream graphic novels for every
age and taste. Staff is superbly
helpful for newbies. *1 Berwick St.*
☎ *020/7437-0187. goshlondon.com.
Tube: Piccadilly Circus. Map p 86.*

★★★ **Smythson of Bond
Street** MAYFAIR   This expensive
and exclusive stationer caters to
generations of posh Londoners,
who would still feel naked without
their Smythson appointment diary.
Also sells elegant leather travel
accessories. *131–132 New Bond St.*
☎ *020/3535-8009. smythson.com.
Tube: Bond St. Map p 86.*

★★ **Stanfords** COVENT GARDEN
In business since 1853, the destination for disoriented travelers has
left its historic home on Long
Acre… but not moved far. Stanfords is London's leading map
store. And if you can't find a guidebook to it here, it likely hasn't been
discovered yet. *7 Mercer Walk.*
☎ *020/7836-1321. stanfords.co.uk.
Tube: Covent Garden. Map p 86.*

★★★ **Waterstones** ST JAMES'S
The flagship branch of the U.K.'s
leading book chain occupies six
floors, making it Europe's largest
bookstore. The choice is enormous.
The top floor has a bar/restaurant
and stunning views of London.
Open till 9pm most days. *203–206
Piccadilly.* ☎ *020/7851-2400.
waterstones.com. Tube: Piccadilly
Circus. Map p 86.*

Waterstones' handsome flagship store.

★★ **Word on the Water**
KING'S CROSS   London's "barge
bookstore" hawks a creative range
of new and used titles from a nar-
rowboat in the shadow of Google's
shiny new London HQ. *Regent's
Canal Towpath.* ☎ *07976/886-982.
wordonthewater.co.uk. Tube: King's
Cross. Map p 86.*

Clothing & Shoes

★★★ **Brick Lane Vintage
Market** EAST END   Not actually
a market but a labyrinthine industrial basement with a whole world
of curated vintage sellers. Expect
anything (and everything) from sunglasses and band T-shirts to Burb-
erry coats. *85 Brick Ln.* ☎ *020/7770-
6028. vintage-market.co.uk. Tube:
Aldgate East. Map p 86.*

★★ **The Cross** NOTTING HILL
Fashionistas in the know come here
for wearable couture from Belle-
rose, Muzungu Sisters, and many
more up-and-coming designers.
You'll also find adorable children's
gifts. *141 Portland Rd.* ☎ *020/7727-
6760. thecrossshop.co.uk. Tube: Holland Park. Map p 85.*

★★ **Fred Perry** SOHO   Petite
home of the famous Laurel Wreath

logo and polos for men and women. A 20th-century style icon that still says Made in England. *12 Newburgh St.* ☎ *020/7734-4494. fredperry.com. Tube: Oxford Circus. Map p 86. Also at Units 6–7 Thomas Neal's, Seven Dials.*

★★ **Jimmy Choo** MAYFAIR U.K. flagship for a London-based global brand that props up the well-tended feet of Oscar contenders and one-percenters. You'll pay dearly for a pair—but they last. *27 New Bond St.* ☎ *020/7493-5858. jimmychoo.com. Tube: Bond St. Map p 86.*

★★ **John Smedley** MAYFAIR Merino woolens and cashmere with Swinging Sixties cachet. Contemporary and timeless lines are always on show. *24 Brook St.* ☎ *020/7495-2222. johnsmedley.com. Tube: Bond St. Map p 86.*

★★ **Luna & Curious** SHOREDITCH Bold, boho and brightly colored threads for trendy kids. All British made. *24–26 Calvert Ave.* ☎ *020/3222-0034. lunaand curious.com. Overground: Shoreditch High St. Map p 86.*

★★ **Nudie Jeans** COVENT GARDEN Sustainability-focused

Gorgeous togs for kids at Luna & Curious.

Swedish brand for organic selvedge denim, plus casual fashions for men and women. *57–59 Monmouth St.* ☎ *020/7836-8040. nudiejeans.com. Tube: Leicester Sq. Map p 86. Also at: 29 D'Arblay St.*

★★ **Pandora Dress Agency** KNIGHTSBRIDGE A big, well-organized consignment store featuring gems (and not just dresses) from big designer names, shoes, and accessories preowned by fashionable Knightsbridge clothes-horses. Expect Celine, Louis Vuitton, and the like. *16–22 Cheval Pl.* ☎ *020/7589-5289. pandoradress agency.com. Tube: Knightsbridge. Map p 85.*

★★ **Primark** SOHO Four-floor behemoth for the U.K.'s leading affordable "fast-fashion" retailer. Menswear, womenswear, beauty products, kids' clothes, travel accessories, and seasonal ranges. Usually open till 10pm. *14–28 Oxford St.* ☎ *020/7580-5510. primark.com. Tube: Tottenham Court Rd. Map p 86.*

★★ **Rokit** EAST END Hipster vintage and big-name brands for a look born in 1980s Camden Market. Everything from blouses and dungarees to classic sunglasses, fridge magnets, and even vintage bridal wear. *101 Brick Ln.* ☎ *020/7375-3864. rokit.co.uk. Tube: Liverpool St. Map p 86.*

★★ **Wax London** SPITALFIELDS The first permanent home for a London brand that's been hoboing around Soho popups since it founded. They zero-in on fresh, smart(-ish) casualwear for men made with ethically sourced fabrics. *105a Commercial St. No phone. waxlondon. com. Tube: Liverpool St. Map p 86.*

Department Stores
★ **Harrods** KNIGHTSBRIDGE From its food halls to its home

Thrifting Done Right

Thrift stores—known here as "charity shops"—are scattered across London. If you have the time and patience to sift, they can reveal bigger bargains than "curated" vintage stores. Thrifting is a sustainable alternative to mass-market fast fashion and most London thrift stores also support charitable causes such as homelessness, overseas aid, or medical research. Quality and range vary by store. However, in general, the more upscale the neighborhood, the more likely you'll find high-quality throwaways (although store staff are increasingly savvy, reducing the chance of a major find). Secondhand books are usually a steal, so long as you aren't stuck on one title or author. Reliable branded chains with multiple outlets—and with a sharper sense of style than your average main-street charity shop—include **Crisis** (crisis.org.uk) and **Traid** (traid.org.uk).

entertainment centers, Harrods is a London institution—as well as over-hyped and overpriced. *87–135 Brompton Rd.* ☎ *020/7730-1234. harrods.com. Tube: Knightsbridge. Map p 85.*

★★ **John Lewis** MARYLEBONE This is *the* place to find homey necessities such as sewing notions, fabrics, and kitchenware, plus lighting and beauty lines. Londoners can't live without it. *300 Oxford St.* ☎ *020/7629-7711. johnlewis.com. Tube: Oxford Circus. Map p 86.*

★★★ **Liberty** SOHO   London's most London department store. Almost everything inside the iconic Tudor Revival building is top-quality without being unapproachably luxe. And if you want Liberty Print, where else to shop but its home? *Regent St. (at Great Marlborough St.).* ☎ *020/3893-3062. libertylondon. com. Tube: Oxford Circus. Map p 86.*

★★★ **Selfridges** MARYLEBONE Inside and out, this grand old department store (opened by a Wisconsiner) is the best in town. Food halls are great; fashions stay forever *à la mode*; and this is the place to buy date-night lingerie or

get a piercing. *400 Oxford St.* ☎ *0800/123-400. selfridges.com. Tube: Marble Arch. Map p 86.*

Food & Drink
★★ **Artisan du Chocolat**
CHELSEA   This award-winning shop creates quirky and delicious flavored chocolates and truffles for the connoisseur. Try a lavender choc—close your eyes, and you're in Provence. *89 Lower Sloane St. No*

Liberty department store.

phone. artisanduchocolat.com. Tube: Sloane Sq. Map p 85.

★★★ Borough Market

BANKSIDE   At this gourmet's paradise, stalls are piled high with free-range meats, cheeses, fruits and veggies, craft beers, and many, many homemade treats. But London's finest food market can be both mouthwateringly delicious and eye-wateringly expensive—offset a little by helping yourself to the many free samples. Closed Mondays. *Southwark St.* ☎ *020/7407-1002. boroughmarket.org.uk. Tube: London Bridge. Map p 86.*

★★ Fortnum & Mason MAYFAIR

The city's ultimate grocer stocks goodies fit for the king—or friends back home—plus gourmet picnic fare and specialty teas. *181 Piccadilly.* ☎ *020/7734-8040. fortnumandmason.com. Tube: Green Park. Map p 86.*

★★ Harrods Food Halls

KNIGHTSBRIDGE   Harrods sells loads of tasty edible gifts branded with its famous name; be sure to ogle the remarkable ceilings in its produce and meat sections. *87–135 Brompton Rd.* ☎ *020/7730-1234. harrods.com. Tube: Knightsbridge. Map p 85.*

★★ Japan Centre ST. JAMES'S

This basement food hall is a Japanophile's dream, overflowing with groceries, teas, sake, and shochu. There's also a sashimi bar and a ramen kitchen. *35a Panton St.* ☎ *0870/820-0055. japancentre.com. Tube: Piccadilly Circus or Leicester Sq. Map p 86.*

★★★ Milroy's of Soho SOHO

Specialist whisky vendor of rare Scotch and special malt bottlings, plus tutored tastings. After dark, pass through a bookcase and down to their old sherry maturation vault for cocktails and, on Mondays, live jazz. *3 Greek St.* ☎ *020/8106-0630.*

Delicious salads at Ottolenghi.

milroys.co.uk. Tube: Tottenham Court Rd. Map p 86.

★★★ Neal's Yard Dairy

BANKSIDE   The best British and Irish farm cheeses of every style, from cow, sheep, or goat milk, and always sold at their peak. They'll pack for home if you ask. (Currently allowed, but customs rules can change: Check dontpackapest. com.) *8 Park St.* ☎ *020/7500-7520. nealsyarddairy.co.uk. Tube: London Bridge. Map p 86.*

★★★ Ottolenghi NOTTING HILL

Small but stacked with exquisite European desserts—English puddings, signature giant meringues, French gâteaux, Italian *torta*, German *bundt*. They also serve boxed salads to go, bursting with the flavors and textures of the Levant. *63 Ledbury Rd.* ☎ *020/7727-1121. ottolenghi.co.uk. Tube: Notting Hill Gate. Map p 85.*

★★ Rococo Chocolates

MARYLEBONE   Chocoholics love this fine store, which sells wittily shaped, high-cocoa-content designer confections and creative flavors (Earl Grey, gingerbread, and more). *3 Moxon St.* ☎ *020/7935-7780. rococochocolates.com. Tube: Baker St. Map p 86.*

Home Decor

★ Cologne & Cotton

MARYLEBONE   Stock up here on elegant bedclothes of pure linen,

Houseware mecca The Conran Shop.

fine fragrances, and cotton sheets in soothing colors and simple designs. The pillowcases are gorgeous. *88 Marylebone High St.* ☎ *020/7486-0595. cologneandcotton.com. Tube: Baker St. Map p 86.*

★ The Conran Shop
MARYLEBONE   Your best bets among a large and varied selection of global designer home merchandise are the kitchenware and bath items. *55 Marylebone High St.* ☎ *020/7723-2233. conranshop. co.uk. Tube: Regent's Park or Baker St. Map p 86.*

★★ Summerill & Bishop
NOTTING HILL   Shop here for sumptuous French housewares, from efficient, humble radiator dusters to the finest table linens and cookware. *100 Portland Rd.* ☎ *020/7221-4566. summerilland bishop.com. Tube: Holland Park. Map p 85.*

Jewelry
★★ Astley Clarke COVENT
GARDEN   Affordable contemporary jewelry and friendly service. Snag yourself (or a loved-one) some Mayfair chic at Midtown prices. *31 Monmouth St.* ☎ *020/ 7479-8720. astleyclarke.com. Tube: Covent Garden. Map p 86.*

★★ Boodles KNIGHTSBRIDGE
One of England's oldest jewelers, founded in 1798, Boodles has

resident designers who keep its collection fresh and modern (not to mention expensive). *6 Sloane St.* ☎ *020/7235-0111. boodles.com. Tube: Knightsbridge. Also at 178 New Bond St. Map p 85.*

★★ Butler & Wilson SOUTH
KENSINGTON   You won't have to remortgage your house to buy the beautiful costume or silver jewelry here. It's *the* best retailer in town for tiaras and brooches. *189 Fulham Rd.* ☎ *020/7352-3045. butterand wilson.co.uk. Tube: S. Kensington. Map p 85.*

★★★ Hirst Collection NOTTING
HILL   Something of a jewelry museum with over 2,000 items, here you'll find extravagant vintage costume baubles from European catwalks of yore, Art Deco pieces, plus interesting affordable and new gems. *59 Pembridge Rd. (at Portobello Rd.). No phone. thehirst collection.com. Tube: Notting Hill Gate. Map p 85.*

Lingerie
★★ Marks & Spencer
MARYLEBONE   This beloved everyday outlet for comfy cotton underwear for men and women has kept up with the times, offering a lot more than old-lady knickers. *458 Oxford St.* ☎ *020/7935-7954. marks andspencer.com. Tube: Marble Arch. Map p 86.*

★★ Rigby & Peller

KNIGHTSBRIDGE   The former corsetiere to the queen specializes in classy underwear, bathing suits (ask for "swimming costumes"), and finely engineered brassieres. Note: Well-made doesn't have to be "sensible." *2 Hans Rd.* ☎ *020/ 7225-4760. rigbyandpeller.com. Tube: Knightsbridge. Map p 85.*

Malls

★★ **Boxpark** SHOREDITCH   Old shipping containers turned tiny stores for urban fashions, pop-ups, one-off accessories, street food, and more. You won't find this stuff anywhere else. *2–10 Bethnal Green Rd. No phone. boxpark.co.uk/ shoreditch. Overground: Shoreditch High St. Map p 86.*

★★ **Coal Drops Yard** KING'S CROSS   Not exactly a mall; more a "gathering" of around 100 boutiques amid postindustrial redevelopment. Every store flashes a little élan, from **Rains** waterproofs to iconic English designs by **Paul Smith**. *Stable St.* ☎ *020/3479-1795.*

kingscross.co.uk/coal-drops-yard. Tube: King's Cross. Map p 86.

★★ Westfield London

SHEPHERDS BUSH   Big European brands—both luxe and Main St.— all under one immaculately designed roof just west of the center. Whether you want beauty products, bags, a Bond watch, or a Bentley automobile, you can buy it here. Dining options aplenty. *Ariel Way.* ☎ *020/3371-2300. westfield. com/united-kingdom/london. Tube/ Overground: Shepherds Bush. Map p 85.*

Markets

★★★ Camden Market

CAMDEN TOWN   It may promote itself as the "capital of alternative London," but this riotous collection of venues (there's no one Camden Market, but rather several stretching along the street and canal), selling art, crafts, jewelry, vintage fashion, clubwear, food, and more, is now one of the capital's top tourist attractions, putting it at the heart of the mainstream. Head to

Market Weekends in the East End

Weekends are a browser's paradise in the area around Spitalfields and Brick Lane. Although some markets stay open (sometimes in low-key fashion) through the week, on Saturdays and Sundays this corner of the East End goes shopaholic. **Spitalfields Old Market** is in full swing and **Petticoat Lane**—founded more than 400 years ago by Huguenot lacemakers who fled Catholic France—spills beyond Wentworth Street with cheap clothes and jewelry. Just east is Brick Lane, the heart of London's Bangladeshi community, where on weekends the **Upmarket** (sundayupmarket.co.uk) surrounds the Old Truman Brewery. A succession of busy, trendy flea markets sells everything from crafts and furniture, vintage clothes, and designer accessories to vinyl records and street food. A 5-minute walk north up Brick Lane takes you to **Columbia Road**'s Sunday-morning flower market and stalls stacked with colorful blooms. All December, it smells of pine sap, cinnamon, and hot chocolate—a festive delight.

The Stables for a more alt-vibe. *Camden High St.* ☎ *020/3763-9900. camdenmarket.com. Tube: Camden Town. Map p 86.*

★★★ Portobello Road Market

NOTTING HILL   Saturday is the best day to join the throngs at the famous antiques market. Most days of the week you'll find all kinds of clothes and food. Friday through Sunday, **Portobello Green** (portobellofashionmarket.co.uk) also has vintage, fashion, and flea market stalls. *Portobello Rd.* ☎ *020/7361-3001. visitportobellocom. Tube: Notting Hill Gate or Ladbroke Grove. Map p 85.*

Museum Shops
★★ kids British Museum

BLOOMSBURY   The B.M. has multiple stores and product ranges, including a "family" shop and a shop stocked with luxury items based on the collections. Its small but excellent bookshop is similarly inspired: If you want a crash course in world history or to learn to read hieroglyphs, they have your back. *Great Russell St.* ☎ *020/7323-8000. britishmuseum.org. Tube: Russell Sq. Map p 86.*

★★ National Gallery Shop

WEST END   This is the city's best source for historical art-related books and stationery. An "on demand" service allows you to purchase a print of any picture in the collection in a size of your choice. *Trafalgar Sq.* ☎ *020/7747-2870. www.nationalgallery.org.uk. Tube: Charing Cross. Map p 86.*

★★ Saatchi Gallery CHELSEA

All manner of books, sketchpads, and primers for visual thinkers and devotees of contemporary aesthetics. *Duke of York's HQ, King's Rd. No phone. saatchistore.com. Tube: Sloane Sq. Map p 85.*

A dinosaur greets young shoppers at Hamleys.

★★ Victoria & Albert Museum

SOUTH KENSINGTON   This must-stop sells everything from post-cards to jewelry inspired by the V&A collection. Cool finds include hand-painted tools and nostalgic toys. *Cromwell Rd.* ☎ *020/7942-2000. vam.ac.uk/south-kensington. Tube: S. Kensington. Map p 85.*

Toys & Games
★★★ kids Forbidden Planet Megastore COVENT GARDEN

A nerd's paradise: F. P. is London's ultimate destination for manga, comics, collectibles, RPG gaming, and themed merch. Browsers spend hours in here. *179 Shaftesbury Ave.* ☎ *020/7420-3666. forbiddenplanet.com. Tube: Tottenham Court Rd. Map p 86.*

★ kids Hamleys SOHO London's

most famous toy store has seven floors of toys, games, tricks, dolls, and more. As you enter, you're greeted by giant-sized cuddly toys. *189–196 Regent St.* ☎ *0371/704-1977. hamleys.com. Tube: Oxford Circus. Map p 86.* ●

5 The **Great Outdoors**

Hyde Park & Kensington Garden⫶

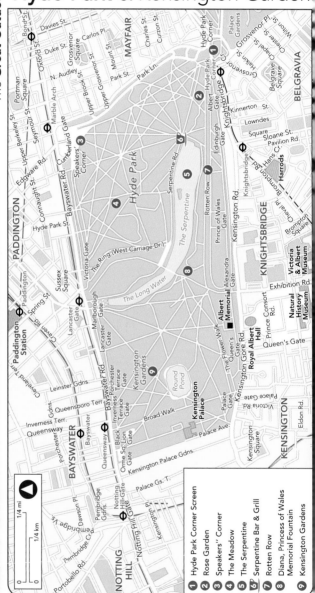

1 Hyde Park Corner Screen
2 Rose Garden
3 Speakers'' Corner
4 The Meadow
5 The Serpentine
6 Serpentine Bar & Grill
7 Rotten Row
8 Diana, Princess of Wales Memorial Fountain
9 Kensington Gardens

Previous page: Boating on the Serpentine in Hyde Park.

Since 1536, when Henry VIII appropriated it as hunting land from the monks of Westminster Abbey, 142-hectare (351-acre) Hyde Park has been the scene of duels, highway robbery, and sports. Today, it is an oasis between some of London's toniest districts. Locals and visitors come to sunbathe, rollerblade, putter around in boats, attend outdoor concerts, and generally leave the noise of the city behind. START: **Tube to Hyde Park Corner.**

1 Hyde Park Corner Screen.
Erected in 1828, this imposing park entrance (one of six) was designed by Decimus Burton, the architect responsible for much of Hyde Park's layout. The triple-arched screen is composed of Ionic columns, bronzed ironwork, and carved friezes inspired by the Elgin Marbles (p 29, **3**). Unfortunately, it's being degraded by air pollution at this busy traffic circle. ⏱ *10 min.*

2 ★ kids Rose Garden. From the Rose Garden, a riot of color in early summer, you can admire the back of Apsley House, former home of (and currently a museum dedicated to) the Duke of Wellington. Nearby stands the Wellington Arch, topped by a majestic statue, *Winged Victory*, erected to commemorate the Iron Duke's numerous military triumphs, notably at Waterloo (1815). The garden is embellished with fountains and climbing-rose trellises, both much loved by kids. Its central fountain is ringed with benches where you can sit with a picnic lunch, as hopeful sparrows flutter. ⏱ *20 min.*

3 ★ Speakers' Corner. The park's northeast corner provides a peculiarly British tribute to free speech. In a tradition upheld since 1872, members of the public can stand here and declaim their heartfelt opinions on whatever they choose—and anyone is allowed to answer back. In the past, you may have heard Karl Marx, the Suffragettes, or George Orwell trying to convert the masses. These days, they would be on social media, too. ⏱ *15 min.*

4 ★★ kids The Meadow. Amid all the neatly tended greenery is something a little more real. A 4-hectare (10-acre) section of the park has been turned into a wild meadow, filled with blooming flowers in summer and home to an assortment of creatures, including songbirds, butterflies, bees, and creepy-crawlies. Themed walks are

Speakers' Corner.

Lily pond in Hyde Park.

offered in summer; check the website for details. ⏱ *30 min. royalparks.org.uk/parks/hyde-park.*

⑤ ★★★ kids The Serpentine. Queen Caroline had the Westbourne River dammed in 1730 to create the Serpentine, a lake upon which she moored two royal yachts. This lovely spot is now the premier boating lake in London for the masses. You can venture out on the water by renting a pedal boat or rowboats from the Boat House on its north edge. The Serpentine Lido is open for outdoor swimming all summer—but the water can be a bit chilly. ⏱ *1 hr. Hourly pedalo rental £12 adults, £6 children, £32 family. Apr–Oct 10am–6pm; Nov–Mar Wed–Sun weather dependent. Full-day swimming £7 adults, £3.50 children, £15 families; heavily discounted price 4–6pm.*

⑥ With the best view over the water, **★ Serpentine Bar & Kitchen** serves hot meals, sandwiches, and drinks (wine included) that are a cut above the usual park cafeteria cuisine. You're welcome to picnic on the tables outside. *Eastern side of the Serpentine.* ☎ *020/7706-8114. £.*

⑦ ★ kids Rotten Row. In the late 1680s, William III ordered 300 lamps to be hung from trees along this 1.5-mile riding path—whose name is probably an English corruption of its original appellation, *Route de Roi* ("King's Road")—in a vain attempt to stop a plague of highwaymen active in the park, and thereby creating the first artificially illuminated road in Britain. The lamps have gone, but the path is still used by riders from local stables. If you want to give it a try, contact **Ross Nye Stables,** 8 Bathurst Mews (rossnyestables. co.uk; ☎ 020/7262-3791). ⏱ *1 hr. Just north of the park, behind Lancaster Gate Tube Station. Private 1-hr ride £90.*

⑧ ★ kids Diana, Princess of Wales Memorial Fountain. This contemporary granite fountain, on the south shore of the Serpentine, was opened by Queen Elizabeth II in 2004. No less dogged by controversy than the tragic princess who inspired it, the 700-ton, £6.5-million fountain has suffered from flooding, closures, and a slippery bottom. Children, who were meant to play happily in its cascading waters, are now restricted to toe-dipping and an occasional splash. ⏱ *20 min. Near the Lido.*

⑨ ★★★ kids Kensington Gardens. Originally a part of Hyde Park, the 111-hectare (274-acre) Kensington Gardens were

partitioned into an exclusive pre-
serve of royalty in the 18th century,
and only opened again to the public in the early 1800s. Originally laid
out in Dutch style (emphasizing
water, avenues, and topiary), these
attractive gardens are popular with
families.

Kensington Gardens Highlights

The bronze **9A** ★★ **kids** **Peter Pan
Statue** was sculpted in 1912 by Sir
George Frampton at the behest of
author J. M. Barrie and is the most
visited landmark in the park. A
short walk north and you arrive at
the **9B** ★ **kids** **Italian Gardens,**
which followed the rage for all
things Italian when they were
crafted in 1861 from Carrara marble
and Portland stone. Generations of
children have floated model boats
on the **9C** ★ **kids** **Round Pond,**
built in 1728. Today you'll see
sophisticated model yachts and
wildfowl. West of the pond is the
9D **Broad Walk.**

Nineteenth-century ladies and gentlemen promenaded along this
tree-lined path past Kensington
Palace and flirted by the Bandstand
(though the current incarnation
dates to 1931). Kids will race on to
the **9E** ★★ **kids** **Diana, Princess
of Wales Memorial Playground,**
centered on a huge wooden pirate
ship. Finish up at Kensington Palace, restored and revamped (p 39,
8) and a well-earned sit-down at
the **9F** ★★ **Pavilion,** where a
good afternoon tea is served.
🕐 *2–3 hr.* ☎ *020/3166-6113.
kensingtonpalacepavilion.co.uk.*

Regent's **Park**

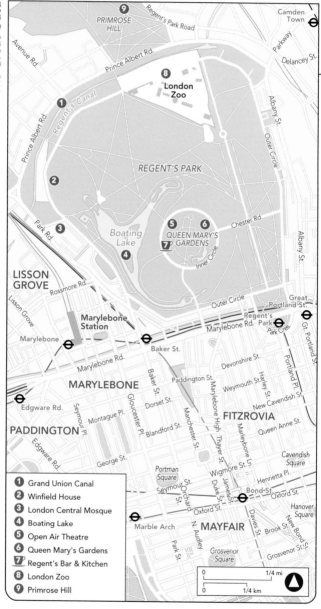

1 Grand Union Canal
2 Winfield House
3 London Central Mosque
4 Boating Lake
5 Open Air Theatre
6 Queen Mary's Gardens
7 Regent's Bar & Kitchen
8 London Zoo
9 Primrose Hill

0   1/4 mi
0   1/4 km

This 160-hectare (4395-acre) gem started out, like so many London parks, as a hunting ground for Henry VIII. It was restyled in the early 19th century by John Nash (1752–1835) following the Romantic ideal of *rus in urbe* ("country in the city"). In truth, the sophistication of its flowerbeds, formal gardens with fountains, and ornamental lake make it much more *urbe* than *rus*. START: **Tube to Camden Town.**

Regent's Canal.

❶ ★★ kids Regent's Canal.

Londoners traveled the city by boat when Regent's Park was in its infancy, and this is your chance to follow in their wake. The Grand Union Canal, opened in 1814, now incorporates 137 miles of waterway connecting the River Thames with the Chiltern Hills in Oxfordshire. Water buses ply the scenic Regent's Canal section (opened in 1820), taking you from Camden Lock's market stalls through the grounds of London Zoo to neighborhoods of grand Victorian houses on either side of the canal path to Little Venice—an area whose name is more aspirational than accurate (there's just the one canal). Stroll back along the

canalside past colorful houseboats for 20 minutes until you spot the minaret. ⏱ *45 min. Camden Lock.* ☎ *020/7482-2550. londonwaterbus. com. One-way tickets £14 adults, £11 seniors, students & children 5–16. Cash not accepted. Book ahead online in summer.*

❷ Winfield House.

As you sail, notice to your left some 4.6-m (15-ft.) high gates protecting a fine mansion beyond. Woolworth heiress Barbara Hutton built this Georgian pile in 1936, adding extensive gardens and trees. A year after World War II, Hutton donated the antiques-filled home to the American government for use as the official residence of the U.S. ambassador. Unfortunately, you must be an invited guest to enter.

❸ ★ London Central Mosque.

The minaret and dome poking above the plane trees, visible from many a local vantage point, belongs to central London's main mosque and Islamic cultural center. It dates to the 1940s, when King George VI laid the first stone. *146 Park Rd.* ☎ *020/7724-3363. iccuk.org.*

❹ ★★ kids Boating Lake.

Operating on a schedule that may vary with the weather, the Boathouse rents pedal boats and rowboats you can take out on this picturesque lake. On any sunny, warm day—whatever the season—this is the ideal angle for a romantic park photo, complete with a fetching backdrop of weeping willows and reed beds. ⏱ *1 hr. Apr–Oct 11am–6pm, weather permitting.*

The **Great Outdoors**

Regent's Park Boating Lake.

Hourly rental £12 adults, £6 children, £32 family.

⑤ ★★ Open Air Theatre. From mid-May to early September, the stage features alfresco concerts, musicals, and plays including Shakespearean comedies. *See p 149.*

⑥ ★★ Queen Mary's Gardens. Laid out in the 1930s, these regal, dog-free gardens lie at the heart of the park's Inner Circle and are a place of enchanting colors, fragrances, and watery vistas. The carefully tended 12,000 blooms of the Rose Garden are especially fabulous in early June. *⏱ 30 min. Inner Circle.*

Food kiosks scattered around Regent's Park offer snacks and drinks. A slightly heartier lunch is available at **17 The Regent's Bar & Kitchen,** which sells hot mains, salads, and sandwiches, as well as wine and beer, which you can enjoy on a lovely terrace. *Queen Mary's Gardens, adjacent to Rose Garden. ☎ 020/7935-5729. £.*

⑧ ★ kids London Zoo. When this former zoology center opened to the public in 1847, many of its captives, such as Jumbo the Elephant (later bought by P. T. Barnum and shipped to the U.S.), became celebrities. High admission charges

make this a must only for diehards. Note, however, that roughly one-sixth of its 650 species are endangered—and a world-renowned breeding program is the only thing preventing their extinction. *⏱ 2 hr., longer for families. Outer Circle, Regent's Park. ☎ 0344/225-1826. londonzoo.org. £31 adults, £28 seniors, £22 children 3–15. Daily 10am–6pm (Sept–Mar closes 5pm).*

⑨ ★★★ kids Primrose Hill. Climb the hill across the road from the zoo for an iconic view across all central London. Locals gather here on sunny evenings and weekends, or whenever there are firework displays, notably New Year's Eve and November 5th. *⏱ 20 min. ●*

Resident giraffes at the London Zoo.

Dining Best Bets

Best **Pub Food**
★★ Anchor & Hope, *36 The Cut* (p 113)

Best **Afternoon Tea**
★★★ Goring Hotel, *Beeston Place* (p 114); or ★★★ The Ritz Palm Court, *150 Piccadilly* (p 114)

Best **Menu from Centuries Past**
★★★ Dinner by Heston Blumenthal, *66 Knightsbridge* (p 115)

Best **South Asian**
★★★ Rambutan, *Storey St.* (p 119)

Best **Steakhouse**
★★★ Hawksmoor, *3 Yeomans Row* (p 116)

Best for **Vegans & Vegetarians**
★★★ Mildreds, *45 Lexington St.* (p 118)

Best for an **Affordable Farm-to-Table Dinner**
★★ Rabbit, *172 Kings Rd.* (p 119)

Best **Tapas**
★★ Barrafina, *43 Drury Ln.* (p 113)

Best for a **Taste of Georgian England**
★★★ Rules, *35 Maiden Lane* (p 120)

Best **View**
★ Oxo Tower Brasserie, *Bargehouse St.* (p 118)

Best **Use of Fire**
★★★ Acme Fire Cult, *Abbot St.* (p 113); or ★★ BRAT, *4 Redchurch St.* (p 115)

Best for a **Splurge**
★★★ CORE by Clare Smyth, *92 Kensington Park Rd.* (p 115)

Best for **Tasting an Old London Lunch**
★★ Goddard's at Greenwich, *22 King William Walk* (p 115)

Best **Greek**
★★ Halepi, *18 Leinster Terrace* (p 116)

Best **Business Lunch**
★★ Gaucho, *19 Swallow St.* (p 116)

Best **Sushi & Sashimi**
★★★ Sachi, *19 Motcomb St.* (p 120)

Best for a **Nose-to-Tail Carnivore**
★★ St. John, *26 St. John St.* (p 120)

Biggest **Bargain**
★★ Café in the Crypt, *Duncannon St.* (p 115); or ★★ Phat Phuc, *151 Sydney St.* (p 119)

Previous page: A waiter serves a couple sitting in the window seats at Paradise Soho.

Notting Hill & Kensington Dining

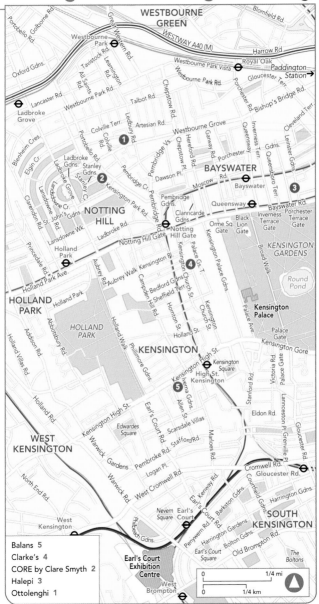

Balans 5
Clarke's 4
CORE by Clare Smyth 2
Halepi 3
Ottolenghi 1

The Best Dining
City & South Bank Dining

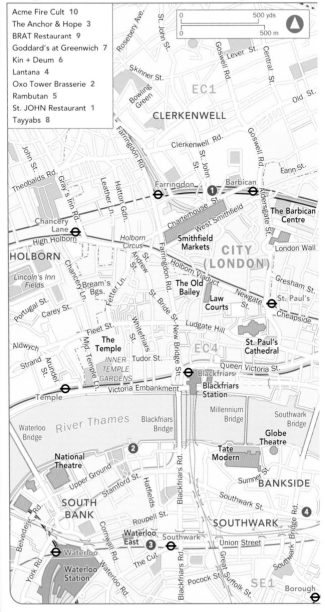

Acme Fire Cult 10
The Anchor & Hope 3
BRAT Restaurant 9
Goddard's at Greenwich 7
Kin + Deum 6
Lantana 4
Oxo Tower Brasserie 2
Rambutan 5
St. JOHN Restaurant 1
Tayyabs 8

0   500 yds
0   500 m

EC1
Rosebery Ave.
St. John St.
Lever St.
Central St.
Goswell Rd.
Skinner St.
Bowling Green
CLERKENWELL
Old St.
Eann St.
Clerkenwell Rd.
St. John St.
Goswell Rd.
John St.
Theobalds Rd.
Gray's Inn Rd.
Leather Ln.
Hatton Gdn.
Farringdon Rd.
Farringdon
Barbican
Aldersgate St.
The Barbican Centre
Chancery Lane
High Holborn
Holborn Circus
Charterhouse St.
West Smithfield
Smithfield Markets
CITY (LONDON)
London Wall
HOLBORN
Lincoln's Inn Fields
Bream's Bgs.
St. Andrew St.
Fetter Ln.
Farringdon Rd.
Holborn Viaduct
The Old Bailey
Law Courts
Newgate St.
Gresham St.
St. Paul's
Cheapside
Portugal St.
Carey St.
Chancery Ln.
Fleet St.
Whitefriars St.
St. Bride St.
New Bridge St.
Ludgate Hill
EC4
St. Paul's Cathedral
Aldwych
Strand
Arundel St.
The Temple
INNER TEMPLE GARDENS
Mid. Temple Ln.
Tudor St.
Queen Victoria St.
Blackfriars
Temple
Victoria Embankment
Blackfriars Station
River Thames
Blackfriars Bridge
Millennium Bridge
Southwark Bridge
Globe Theatre
Waterloo Bridge
National Theatre
Upper Ground
Tate Modern
Sumner St.
BANKSIDE
SOUTH BANK
Stamford St.
Hatfields
Blackfriars Rd.
Southwark St.
Belvedere Rd.
Roupell St.
SOUTHWARK
Southwark Bridge Rd.
York Rd.
Waterloo
Cornwall Rd.
Waterloo East
The Cut
Waterloo Rd.
Southwark
Union Street
SE1
Great Suffolk St.
Waterloo Station
Pocock St.
Borough

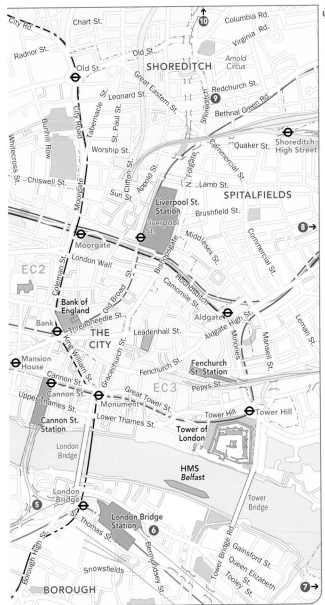

West End Dining

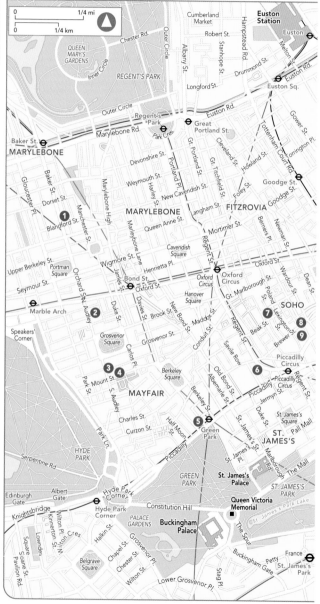

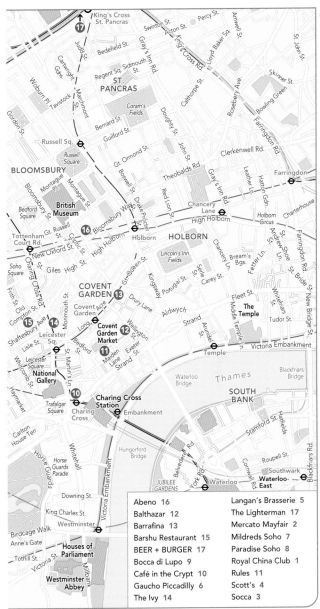

Abeno 16
Balthazar 12
Barrafina 13
Barshu Restaurant 15
BEER + BURGER 17
Bocca di Lupo 9
Café in the Crypt 10
Gaucho Piccadilly 6
The Ivy 14

Langan's Brasserie 5
The Lighterman 17
Mercato Mayfair 2
Mildreds Soho 7
Paradise Soho 8
Royal China Club 1
Rules 11
Scott's 4
Socca 3

Knightsbridge & Chelsea Dining

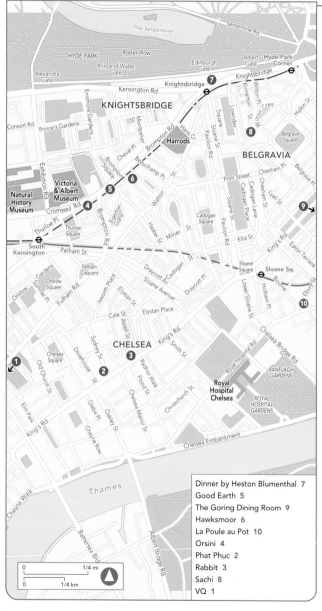

Dinner by Heston Blumenthal 7
Good Earth 5
The Goring Dining Room 9
Hawksmoor 6
La Poule au Pot 10
Orsini 4
Phat Phuc 2
Rabbit 3
Sachi 8
VQ 1

London Restaurants A to Z

★★ kids **Abeno** BLOOMSBURY
JAPANESE This tiny Japanese
eatery specializes in *okonomi-yaki*,
something between a giant omelet
and a pancake loaded with meat
and fresh vegetables. Choose your
ingredients and cook everything
yourself at the *teppan* (hotplate)
installed in each table. Familiar sides
like gyoza and noodle dishes are
also available—but much less fun.
47 Museum St. ☎ *020/7405-3211.
abeno.co.uk. Main courses £16–£35.
Lunch & dinner Mon–Sat. Tube: Holborn or Tottenham Ct. Rd. Map p 110.*

★★★ **Acme Fire Cult** DALSTON
MODERN BBQ Global culinary
influences, intense flavors, and
everything cooked over a fire then
served at casual seating, with the
best perches on a covered all-year
terrace. Smoke wafts, music is loud,
and the sharing plates—especially
vegetable dishes—really sing. Book
ahead. *The Bootyard, Abbot St.
acmefirecult.com. Main courses £19–
£27. Lunch & dinner Thurs–Sat, dinner Tues & Wed, lunch Sun.
Overground: Dalston Junction or
Dalston Kingsland. Map p 108.*

★★ **Anchor & Hope** SOUTH
BANK *MODERN BRITISH*
A stripped-back pub serves
Mediterranean-tinged British food
that's similarly stripped back to its flavors: big, bold, seasonal, and contemporary. The menu changes daily.
36 The Cut. ☎ *020/7928-9898. anchor
andhopepub.co.uk. Main courses £19–
£26. Lunch Wed–Sun, dinner Mon–
Sat. Tube: Southwark. Map p 108.*

★ kids **Balans** KENSINGTON
INTERNATIONAL A reasonably
priced and varied menu make this a
reliable microchain for all-day dining, on big or small plates, and
even a wide choice of cocktails. *187
Kensington High St.* ☎ *020/7376-
0115. balans.co.uk. Main courses
£14–£25. Breakfast, lunch & dinner
daily (closes early Sun). Tube: High
St. Kensington. Map p 107.*

★★ **Balthazar** COVENT GARDEN
FRENCH Cutlery clanks and jazz
plays at this bustling brasserie. An
ever-popular classic Parisian *prix-fixe*
lunch and pre-theater menu (Mon–
Fri) is the value choice—reservations
are highly recommended. *4–6 Russell St.* ☎ *020/3301-1155. balthazar
london.com. Main courses £13–£29;
set lunch & pre-theater £25/£28 for
2/3 courses. Lunch & dinner daily.
Tube: Covent Garden. Map p 110.*

★★ **Barrafina** COVENT GARDEN
SPANISH Countertop seating for

Grilling is serious business at Acme Fire Cult.

Transporting Teatimes

Afternoon tea is an overpriced tourist pursuit, to be sure, but that doesn't mean it's not delightful to pass the time pretending to be fancy. Arrive hungry to maximize your return from a never-ending banquet of scones, clotted cream, pastries, light sandwiches, and a bottomless brewed torrent. Dress up, if you please, and be discreet about the Insta-shots. Among the most legendary, best-located afternoon teas, are **Brown's Hotel** (roccofortehotels. com; ☎ 020/7518-4006; £75), a Mayfair institution open since 1837; **The Goring** (thegoring.com; ☎ 020/7769-4485; £75), near Buckingham Palace and serving on bespoke canary-yellow china; the **Lanesborough** (lanesborough.com; ☎ 020/7259-5599; £75), dazzling in every way, from the delicacy of the pastry to the Regency frills of the conservatory glass; and the **Ritz** (theritzlondon.com; ☎ 020/7300-2345; £72), where you'll need to book weeks ahead to experience the Palm Court's gilding, mirrors, and boisterous flower arrangements. Note that most places run several sittings per afternoon and will allow—nay, encourage—you to upgrade your tea with a glass of bubbly. With upscale accommodation rates now putting these magnificent hotels out of reach for most travelers, this can be a fun, relatively affordable way to experience them.

—Jason Cochran, Editor-in-Chief, Frommers.com

a timeless tapas bar-restaurant that's always packed: Reserve ahead. Seafood and Iberico pork are consistently on point and the Spanish wine and sherry list is exceptional. *43 Drury Ln. No phone. barrafina.co.uk. Dishes £8–£19. Lunch Tues–Sat, dinner daily. Tube: Covent Garden or Holborn. Map p 110.*

★★ **Barshu** SOHO *SZECHUAN* Spicy Szechuan cooking at its most dependable, even if some of the dishes—like dry-wok pig's intestines—may require a leap of faith from the uninitiated. It has plenty of traditional Chinese and vegetarian choices, too, as well as whole roasted fish. *28 Frith St. barshurestaurant.co.uk. Main courses £15–£21. Lunch & dinner daily. Tube: Leicester Sq. Map p 110.*

★★ kids **Beer + Burger** KING'S CROSS *BURGER BAR* Need we

elaborate? There's shared bench seating, 20 beer taps, sloppy burgers, neon, and lots of noise. It's not romantic, but everything is griddled fresh and tastes great. *1 York Way. ☎ 020/3963-5795. beerandburger store.com. Burgers £11–£15. Lunch & dinner daily. Tube: King's Cross. Map p 110.*

★★ **Bocca di Lupo** SOHO *MODERN ITALIAN* Classic trattoria flavors from across Italy get refined on a daily changing menu that ebbs and flows with the seasons—from winter artichokes through stuffed zucchini flowers in spring to summer asparagus and fall mushrooms. *12 Archer St. ☎ 020/7734-2223. boccadilupo. com. Main courses £18–£30; set 2-course lunch (Mon–Fri) £15. Lunch & dinner daily. Tube: Piccadilly Circus. Map p 110.*

Dining underground at Café in the Crypt.

★★★ BRAT SHOREDITCH

BASQUE BBQ   The vibe is rustic and casual but the bold, Basque-influenced cookery—over an open-flame grill—is 150% serious. The best approach is to order a few seasonal plates to share; perhaps a whole John Dory, mutton chop, spider crab toast, wood-roasted greens, and smoked potatoes. *4 Redchurch St. No phone. bratrestaurant.co.uk. Main courses £21–£31. Lunch & dinner daily. Overground: Shoreditch High St. Map p 108.*

★★ kids Café in the Crypt

SOHO BRITISH DINER   One of the center's best bargains, this subterranean cafeteria offers cheap, hearty meals, as well as a jolly good tea. There's outdoor terrace seating in summer and weekly live jazz (pre-booking recommended). Cash not accepted. *St. Martin-in-the-Fields Church, Duncannon St. 020/7766-1158. stmartin-in-the-fields.org. Main courses £10–£14. Breakfast, lunch & afternoon tea daily, dinner Fri & Sat. Tube: Charing Cross. Map p 110.*

★★★ CORE by Clare Smyth

NOTTING HILL CONTEMPORARY BRITISH   The home-base of a former winner of World's Best Female Chef has captured every award going. Each mouthful journeys through the very best British ingredients, combined and presented in uniquely creative ways. A visit here is the ultimate, unforgettable romantic splurge—reserve well ahead. *92 Kensington Park Rd. 020/3937-5086. corebyclare smyth.com. Menus £155–£225. Lunch Thurs–Sat, dinner Tues–Sat. Tube: Notting Hill Gate. Map p 107.*

★★ kids Goddard's at Greenwich GREENWICH PIE & MASH

A proper taste of old London, such "pie-and-mash shops" are disappearing fast. This casual, family-run joint serves the traditional menu of minced meat pie, mashed potato, and gravy or parsley liquor, with jellied eel on the side. Newfangled vegetarian and gluten-free pies are also offered. *22 King William Walk, Greenwich. 020/8305-9612. goddardsatgreenwich.co.uk. Main courses £6–£8. Lunch & dinner daily. DLR: Cutty Sark. Map p 108.*

★★★ Clarke's KENSINGTON

MODERN EUROPEAN   Californiainfluenced chef Sally Clarke gratifies refined tastebuds in her charming dining room, with a focus on the freshest produce in ingredient-led, monthly-changing dishes. There's an onsite shop and bakery. *124 Kensington Church St. 020/7221-9225. sallyclarke.com/restaurant. Main courses £44–£48; 3-course set lunch £38. Lunch & dinner Tues–Sat. Tube: Notting Hill Gate. Map p 107.*

★★★ Dinner by Heston Blumenthal KNIGHTSBRIDGE

CONTEMPORARY BRITISH   When Britain's "culinary scientist" Heston Blumenthal serves up traditional fare, he really means it, with recipes

"Meat Fruit" at Dinner by Heston Blumenthal.

scoured from the history books and reinvented. Tuck into the charmingly named "Rice & Flesh" (calf sweetbreads, saffron, and red wine), served to King Richard II in 1390 or "Meat Fruit" (from 1500), chicken liver parfait dressed convincingly as a mandarin orange. Book online and well ahead. *Inside Mandarin Oriental Hyde Park, 66 Knightsbridge.* ☎ *020/7201-3833. dinnerbyheston. co.uk. Main courses £48–£64; 3-course lunch £59. Lunch & dinner daily. Tube: Knightsbridge. Map p 112.*

★★ kids Gaucho WEST END
ARGENTINE Consistently good Argentine dining in London—which means well-sourced meat with a side of meat: grilled beef every which way, churrasco, lomo, and more, plus an outstanding Argentine wine list. This is the toniest branch of what's now a minichain with 12 London locations. Gaucho is also a slam dunk for a business lunch. *25 Swallow St.* ☎ *020/7734-4040. gauchorestaurants.com. Main courses £18–£50; lunch menu £27/£30 for 2/3 courses. Lunch & dinner daily. Tube: Piccadilly Circus. Map p 110.*

★ kids The Good Earth
KNIGHTSBRIDGE *CHINESE* More elegant than your usual Chinese restaurant, with prices to match, this longstanding Knightsbridge favorite does a great crispy aromatic duck. It's good for vegetarians, too.

233 Brompton Rd. ☎ *020/7584-3658. goodearthgroup.co.uk. Main courses £19–£36. Lunch & dinner daily. Tube: Knightsbridge or S. Kensington. Map p 112.*

★★★ The Goring Dining Room
VICTORIA *BRITISH* Mutton broth, cured trout, roast grouse, saltmarsh lamb, an iconic lobster omelet, and rice pudding: You can't get more English than the menu at the Goring, a hotel whose restaurant recalls Edwardian elegance at its finest. *15 Beeston Place.* ☎ *020/7769-4475. thegoring.com. Main courses £38–£50; Breakfast & dinner daily; lunch Sun–Fri. Tube: Victoria. Map p 112.*

★★ kids Halepi BAYSWATER
GREEK Bring the whole family to share classic home-style Greek taverna dishes and simple Mediterranean grilled fish and meat. The baklava is among the best around. Halepi is small and popular: Reserve ahead. *18 Leinster Terrace.* ☎ *020/7262-1070. halepi-restaurant. co.uk. Main courses £15–£30. Lunch & dinner daily. Tube: Bayswater or Queensway. Map p 107.*

★★★ Hawksmoor KNIGHTS-
BRIDGE *STEAKHOUSE* London's best steaks—from rump to premium cuts—are joined by a supporting cast of hearty appetizers, grilled fish, classic sides, and well-crafted cocktails. Now at 8 London locations. Lunch and pre-theater menus are a steal. *3 Yeomans Row.* ☎ *020/7590-9290. thehawksmoor.com. Main courses £29–£45; lunch/pre-theater Mon–Sat £27/£31 for 2/3 courses. Lunch & dinner daily. Tube: S. Kensington or Knightsbridge. Map p 112.*

★★ The Ivy COVENT GARDEN
MODERN EUROPEAN The menu is surprisingly diverse (from caviar to Iberico pork chops to irresistible English puddings) at this longstanding haunt of theatrical celebs and their agents. For a fancy place,

Hawksmoor restaurant.

it's not overpriced, especially the fixed-price menu (Mon–Fri 2:30–6pm). *1–5 West St.* ☎ *020/7836-4751. the-ivy.co.uk. Main courses £17–£36; set menu £26.50/£31.50 for 2/3 courses. Lunch & dinner daily. Tube: Leicester Sq. Map p 110.*

★★ **Kin + Deum** LONDON BRIDGE *THAI* Homestyle Bangkok cuisine is the inspiration behind everything from the food to the friendly, family welcome. Knock yourself out with Thai classics like *som tum* (spicy-sour papaya salad) or Bangkok's *gra pow* (stir-fried pork with Thai basil). *2 Crucifix Ln.* ☎ *020/7357-7995. kindeum.com. Main courses £13.50–£19. Lunch & dinner daily. Tube: London Bridge. Map p 108.*

★ **Lantana** BANKSIDE *AUSTRALIAN* There's poke, noodles, and fresh Pacific flavors aplenty on the menu here. But Lantana's rep is founded on its popular weekend brunch, for which you'll need to book ahead. Go bottomless with or without 90 minutes of Mimosas. *44–46 Southwark St.* ☎ *020/7403-2633. lantanacafe. co.uk. Main courses £15–£20; bottomless weekend brunch £39/£46. Breakfast, lunch & dinner Tues–Sat, breakfast & lunch Sun–Mon. Tube: London Bridge or Southwark. Map p 108.*

★★ **La Poule au Pot** BELGRAVIA *FRENCH* This chic retro French bistro brings a slice of rural France to posh Chelsea and Belgravia. The romantic atmosphere, friendly staff, and rustic dishes always make eating here a joy. House wines are dangerously drinkable. *231 Ebury St.*

Money-Saving Fine Dining

To bag a top meal at an affordable price, check a restaurant's website for set-price deals, usually on a weekday lunchtime or the pre-theater slot. (You'll then need iron discipline to avoid being sucked into à la carte and/or celebrating your thrift with a signature cocktail.) London's weekday newspaper, the **Evening Standard** (standard.co.uk), often runs dining promotions. It's worth bookmarking **TimeOut** (timeout.com/London/foodanddrink) and **Secret London** (secretldn.com) for the skinny on openings and deals. *Note:* All prices displayed on a menu or advertisement **must include** VAT (i.e. sales tax). The restaurant may add a 12% to 15% service charge, which is optional but should go to waitstaff (check with your server). If no service is levied, a standard tip in London is 10% to 15%.

Dover sole at La Poule Au Pot.

☎ 020/7730-7763. pouleaupot.co.uk. Main courses £23–£41. Lunch & dinner daily. Tube: Sloane Sq. Map p 112.

★★ kids The Lighterman

KING'S CROSS *GASTROPUB* The light-drenched location, with terrace seating in the heart of the massive postindustrial King's Cross development, could hardly be better. The menu is short and nails gastropub fare like Cornish mussels steamed in apple cider with samphire. *3 Granary Sq.* ☎ 020/3846-3400. thelighterman.co.uk. Main courses £18–£28. Lunch & dinner daily. Tube: King's Cross. Map p 110.

★★ Mercato Mayfair MAYFAIR

STREET FOOD Three floors of street food, beer, and craft cocktails inside a stunning deconsecrated Neoclassical church. Thai, Malaysian, Italian, shellfish, bao buns, and more presented with the kind of flair you'd expect of such a bougie neighborhood. *St. Mark's, N. Audley St. No phone.* mercatometropolitano. com/mercato-mayfair. Main courses £8–£18. Breakfast, lunch & dinner daily. Tube: Bond St. Map p 110.

★★ kids Mildreds SOHO

VEGETARIAN/VEGAN A Soho institution, with affordable, 100% plant-based international food including South Asian and Middle Eastern dishes, burgers, salads, and juices. Don't skip the tasty desserts. *45 Lexington St.* ☎ 020/7494-1634. mildreds.co.uk. Main courses £15–£17.

Breakfast, lunch & dinner Mon–Sat. Tube: Piccadilly Circus or Oxford Circus. Map p 110.

★★★ Ottolenghi NOTTING

HILL *MEDITERRANEAN* The first of now five branches strewn across town, this cafe and deli posts a fresh, Eastern Mediterranean–inspired menu at 11am daily. The food is based around healthy and imaginatively prepared salads and light, flavorsome cakes. There's one communal table—and this is probably London's best takeout box lunch. *63 Ledbury Rd.* ☎ 020/7727-1121. ottolenghi.co.uk. Lunch menu (2–4 dishes) £16.50–£22.50. Breakfast & lunch daily. Tube: Bayswater or Notting Hill Gate. Map p 107.

★ Oxo Tower Brasserie SOUTH

BANK *INTERNATIONAL* You'll want to come here in summer for a table on their panoramic balcony: Enjoy the best river views in London while sampling dishes that fuse Mediterranean, French, and British influences. *Oxo Tower Wharf, Bargehouse St.* ☎ 020/7803-3888. oxotowerrestaurant.com. Main courses £23–£43. Lunch & dinner daily. Tube: Blackfriars. Map p 108.

★★ Paradise Soho SOHO *SRI*

LANKAN Imaginative modern Sri Lankan small plates paired with cocktails inspired by the food's seasonal

Mercato Mayfair.

Mildreds staff taking a breather.

British ingredients. Their devilled shrimp with *malu-miris* capsicum redefines the term *fiery. 61 Rupert St. paradisesoho.com. Main courses £14–£25. Lunch Tues–Sat, dinner Mon–Sat. Tube: Piccadilly Circus. Map p 110.*

★★ Phat Phuc CHELSEA
VIETNAMESE/SINGAPOREAN
Value and flavor stand out in a neighborhood now dominated by chains. Aromas of *pho* and *laksa* drift streetward from the covered outdoor terrace. No reservations. *151 Sydney St. ☎ 020/7351-3843. phatphucnoodle bar.co.uk. Main courses £10–£12. Lunch & early dinner daily. Tube: S. Kensington or Sloane Sq. Map p 112.*

★★ Rabbit CHELSEA
CONTEMPORARY BRITISH Come for the zero-waste, field-to-fork

credentials: Most of the meat comes from the owners' family farm and foraging is another common source. You'll be back for creative seasonal dishes such as lamb rump with spring onions and oyster mushrooms. *172 Kings Rd. ☎ 020/3750-0172. rabbit-restaurant.com. Main courses £15–£30; set lunch (Mon–Fri) £22/£25 for 2/3 courses. Lunch Tues–Sun, dinner daily. Tube: Sloane Sq. Map p 112.*

★★★ Rambutan BANKSIDE *SRI LANKAN* "Sri Lankan diaspora"
cooking in clay pots and over an open fire. This place made an instant splash on opening in 2023 with vibrant meat and seafood dishes. Tempered turmeric potatoes somehow pack insane levels of flavor into the humble tuber. Ask for ground-floor seating; cashless payments only. *10 Stoney St. No phone. ram-butanlondon.com. Main courses £11–£17. Lunch Wed–Sat, dinner Tues–Sat. Tube: London Bridge. Map p 108.*

★★ Royal China Club MARYLE-
BONE *CHINESE* This is the real deal for dim sum, with the choice and quality you'd find in Hong Kong. Evening is for upscale Cantonese dishes, strong on seafood specialties. *40–42 Baker St. ☎ 020/7486-3898. royalchinagroup.co.uk. Main courses £19–£48 (dim sum £7–£12). Lunch & dinner daily. Tube: Baker St. Map p 110.*

Outdoor seating at Oxo Tower Brasserie.

The Best Dining

★★★ **Rules** COVENT GARDEN *TRADITIONAL ENGLISH* The most traditional Olde English restaurant in London, Rules dates back to 1798, and is a must for Anglophile lovers of game, Scottish salmon, steak and kidney pies, and traditional English puddings. The cozy Winter Garden bar upstairs serves classic predinner cocktails. *35 Maiden Ln.* ☎ 020/7836-5314. *rules.co.uk. Main courses £23–£34. Lunch & dinner daily. Tube: Covent Garden or Leicester Sq. Map p 110.*

★★ **St. John** CLERKENWELL *MODERN BRITISH* Inside a former smokehouse, just a hoof's throw from Smithfield Meat Market, this is a carnivore's delight—founder chef Fergus Henderson is famed for using every part of the animal (aka "nose-to-tail" eating). Dishes like lamb offal with broad beans may not be for everyone, but food writers have been raving since 1994. Roast bone marrow is a knockout. *26 St. John St.* ☎ 020/7251-0848. *stjohnrestaurant.com. Main courses £22–£34. Lunch daily, dinner Mon–Sat. Tube: Farringdon. Map p 108.*

★★★ **Sachi** BELGRAVIA *JAPANESE* Nordic-inspired Japanese dishes here are way more than just Instagrammable beauties. Both the charcoal-grilled mains and chef-selected sashimi exhibit precision and total clarity of flavor. A specialist sake sommelier is the cream on top. *19 Motcomb St.* ☎ 020/7034-5405. *pantechnicon.com/sachi. Main courses £24–£32 (wagyu £52–£90). Lunch & dinner daily. Tube: Knightsbridge. Map p 112.*

★★ **Scott's** MAYFAIR *SEAFOOD* With a show-stopping Busby Berkeley arrangement of crustaceans as its centerpiece, this is one of London's finest fish restaurants. Menu highlights include sauteed razor clams, Dover sole meunière, and beluga caviar blinis with crème fraiche (a mere £255 for 30g/1 oz). *20 Mount St.* ☎ 020/7495-7309. *scotts-mayfair.com. Main courses £25–£42. Lunch & dinner daily. Tube: Bond St. Map p 110.*

★★ **Socca** MAYFAIR *PROVENÇAL* A light-filled dining room is matched by equally fresh and elegant cooking inspired by the flavors of the Côte d'Azur and executed under the watchful eye of multi-award winner Claude Bosi. *41A S. Audley St.* ☎ 020/3376-0000. *soccabistro.com. Main courses £20–£52. Lunch & dinner daily. Tube: Bond St. Map p 110.*

★★ **Tayyabs** EAST END *INDIAN* A little off the beaten track, but ferociously popular, with peak-time lines. Londoners are drawn by expertly spiced grills, dhal, and curries at keen prices. Decor is a little ragged in places, but this place is about flavor, not frills. *83–89 Fieldgate St.* ☎ 020/7247-9543. *tayyabs.co.uk. Main courses £11–£21. Lunch & dinner daily. Tube: Whitechapel. Map p 108.*

★ **kids** **VQ** CHELSEA *DINER* The best reason to come to this busy diner is that it's always open, serving 24/7 breakfast, American comfort food, and tasty brasserie staples to jet-lagged insomniacs and after-hours clubbers. *325 Fulham Rd.* ☎ 020/7376-7224. *vqrestaurants.com. Main courses £12.50–£21. Open 24 hr. Tube: S. Kensington or W. Brompton. Map p 112.* ●

A tasty spread at Tayyabs.

Nightlife Best Bets

Best **Dance Club**
★★★ Fabric, *77a Charterhouse St.*
(p 132)

Best **Wine Bar**
★★★ Gordon's, *47 Villiers St.*
(p 130); or ★★ Cecilia's Wine
House, *42 Drury Ln. (p 130)*

Best **Jazz Club**
★★★ Ronnie Scott's, *47 Frith St.*
(p 134)

Most **Wacky Decor**
★★ Calcooh Callay,
65 Rivington St. (p 130)

Most **Unpretentious Clubbing**
★★ Corsica Studios,
4–5 Elephant Rd. (p 132)

Best for **Drinking in Peace**
★★ The Lamb, *98 Lamb's
Conduit St. (p 137)*

Best **Views**
★★ Sky Garden, *1 Sky Garden
Walk (p 131)*; or Bussey Building
Rooftop Bar, *133 Rye Ln. (p 133)*

Most **Historic Pub**
★★★ Ye Olde Cheshire Cheese,
145 Fleet St. (p 139)

Best for **Blues**
★★ Ain't Nothin' But…,
20 Kingly St. (p 129)

Best **West End Pub**
★★★ The Harp, *47 Chandos Place
(p 137)*; or ★★ The Lyric,
37 Great Windmill St. (p 137)

Best **City Pub**
★★★ The Counting House, *50
Cornhill (p 136)*; or ★★★ The Black
Friar, *174 Queen Victoria St. (p 140)*

Best for **Watching the Game**
★ Bar Kick, *127 Shoreditch High St.*
(p 129)

Best **LGBT Venue**
★★ Heaven, *Villiers St. (p 133)*

Most **Stylish Cocktail Lounge**
★★★ Blue Bar, *Berkeley Hotel,
Wilton Pl. (p 129)*

Best **Hotel Bar**
★★★ The Connaught Bar,
Connaught Hotel, Carlos Pl. (p 130)

Best **Cocktails**
★★ 69 Colebrooke Row,
69 Colebrooke Row (p 129)

Best for **Craft Beer Lovers**
Bermondsey Beer Mile *(p 133)*; or
★★ The Rake, *14 Winchester
Walk (p 130)*

Best **Sound System**
★★ Ministry of Sound,
103 Gaunt St. (p 133); or
★★ Spiritland, *9–10 Stable St.*
(p 132)

Most **Atmospheric Music
Venue**
★★ The Roundhouse, *Chalk Farm
Rd. (p 135)*

Best for a **Pint of Guinness**
★★ The Toucan, *19 Carlisle St.*
(p 137)

Previous Page: The staff at Artesian toast life.

Camden & Angel Nightlife

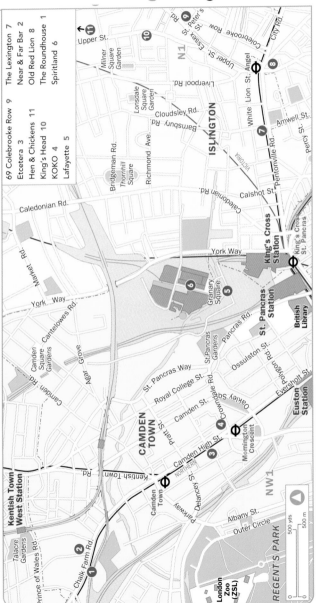

69 Colebrooke Row 9
Etcetera 3
Hen & Chickens 11
King's Head 10
KOKO 4
Lafayette 5

The Lexington 7
Near & Far Bar 2
Old Red Lion 8
The Roundhouse 1
Spiritland 6

West End Nightlife

0 ____ 1/4 mi
0 ____ 1/4 km

Cumberland Market
Euston Station
Euston
Chester Rd
Outer Circle
Albany St.
Robert St.
Hampstead Rd.
Stanhope St.
Melton St.

QUEEN MARY'S GARDENS
REGENT'S PARK
Inner Circle
Drummond St.
Longford St.
Euston Rd.
Euston Sq.
Gower St.

Outer Circle
Regent's Park
Euston Rd.
Great Portland St.
Tottenham Court Rd.
Torrington Pl.

Baker St.
MARYLEBONE
Marylebone Rd.
Park Cres.
Cleveland St.
Howland St.
Goodge St.
Goodge St.

Gloucester Pl.
Baker St.
Dorset St.
Devonshire St.
Weymouth St.
Harley St.
New Cavendish St.
Portland Pl.
Gt. Portland St.
Gt. Titchfield St.
Foley St.
Berners Pl.
Newman St.

Blandford St.
Manchester St.
Marylebone High
MARYLEBONE
Queen Anne St.
Langham St.
Mortimer St.
FITZROVIA

Upper Berkeley St.
Portman Square
Wigmore St.
Henrietta Pl.
Cavendish Square
Regent St.
Oxford St.
Wardour St.
Dean St.

Seymour St.
Orchard St.
James St.
Bond St.
Oxford St.
Oxford Circus
Oxford Circus
Gt. Marlborough St.
Poland St.
Lexington St.
SOHO

Marble Arch
Duke St.
Davies St.
Brook St.
New Bond St.
Hanover Square
Maddox St.
Regent St.
Beak St.
Brewer St.

Speakers' Corner
N. Audley St.
Grosvenor Square
Grosvenor St.
Conduit St.
Savile Row
Piccadilly Circus
Piccadilly Circus

Park St.
Mount St.
Carlos Pl.
S. Audley St.
MAYFAIR
Berkeley Square
Old Bond St.
Albemarle St.
Piccadilly
Jermyn St.
Regent St.

Charles St.
Curzon St.
Hall Moon St.
Berkeley St.
St. James's St.
Duke St.
St. James's Square
Pall Mall

HYDE PARK
Park Ln.
Piccadilly
Green Park
St. James's St.
St. James's Pl.
Marlborough Rd.
The Mall
ST. JAMES'S

Serpentine Rd.
GREEN PARK
St. James's Palace
ST. JAMES'S PARK
St. James's Park Lake

Edinburgh Gate
Albert Gate
Hyde Park Corner
Hyde Park Corner
Constitution Hill
Queen Victoria Memorial
The Spur

Knightsbridge
Wilton Pl.
Kinnerton St.
Wilton Cres.
PALACE GARDENS
Buckingham Palace
Buckingham Gate
Petty France
St. James's Park

Lowndes Square
Sloane St.
Pavilion Rd.
Halkin St.
Chapel St.
Grosvenor Pl.
Stag Pl.

Belgrave Square
Chester St.
Wilton St.
Lower Grosvenor Pl.

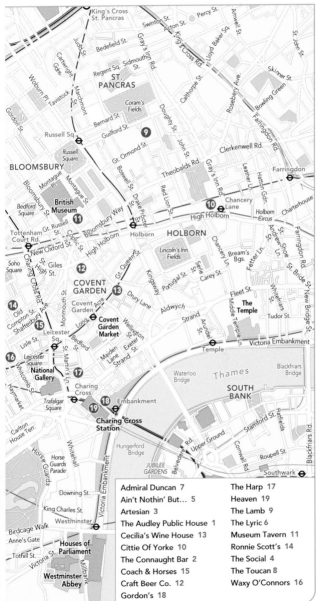

Admiral Duncan 7	The Harp 17
Ain't Nothin' But... 5	Heaven 19
Artesian 3	The Lamb 9
The Audley Public House 1	The Lyric 6
Cecilia's Wine House 13	Museum Tavern 11
Cittie Of Yorke 10	Ronnie Scott's 14
The Connaught Bar 2	The Social 4
Coach & Horses 15	The Toucan 8
Craft Beer Co. 12	Waxy O'Connors 16
Gordon's 18	

City, East End & Bankside Nightlife

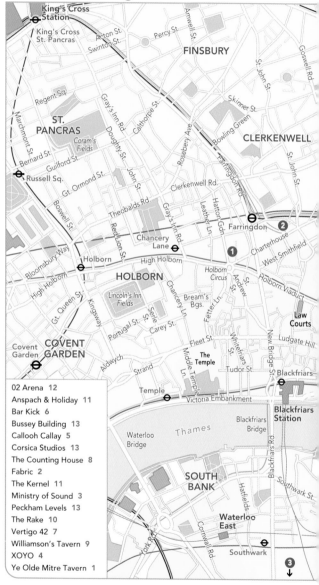

02 Arena 12
Anspach & Holiday 11
Bar Kick 6
Bussey Building 13
Callooh Callay 5
Corsica Studios 13
The Counting House 8
Fabric 2
The Kernel 11
Ministry of Sound 3
Peckham Levels 13
The Rake 10
Vertigo 42 7
Williamson's Tavern 9
XOYO 4
Ye Olde Mitre Tavern 1

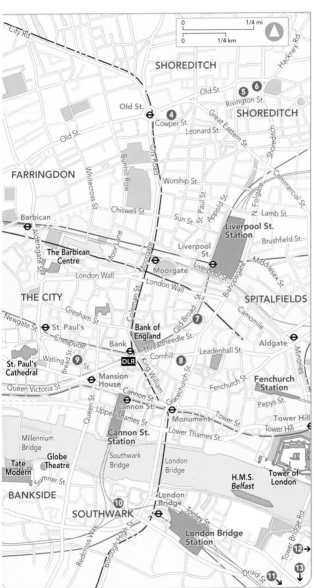

Nightlife in Knightsbridge, Kensington & Chelsea

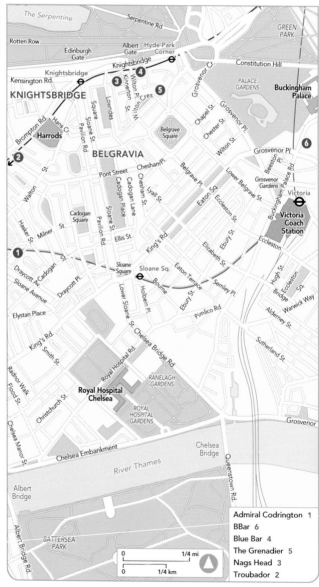

Admiral Codrington 1
BBar 6
Blue Bar 4
The Grenadier 5
Nags Head 3
Troubador 2

London Nightlife A to Z

Enjoying fine spirits at 69 Colebrook Row.

Bars

★★ 69 Colebrooke Row

ANGEL   Billed as "The Bar with No Name," this place has an on-trend speakeasy ambience, with a house jazz pianist, low lighting, and limited capacity—just 30 seats. Cocktails are multi-award-winning and the vibe just the right side of illicit. *69 Colebrook Row.* ☎ *07540/ 528-593. 69colebrookerow.com. Tube: Angel. Map p 123.*

★★ Ain't Nothin' But... SOHO

This tiny joint plucked straight from the bayou may not be Bourbon Street, but it offers live blues every night of the week. *20 Kingly St.* ☎ *020/7287-0514. Tube: Piccadilly Circus or Oxford Circus. Map p 124.*

★★ Artesian MARYLEBONE

Swanky and expensive, Artesian has some of the most opulent decor this side of royalty; the interior is a riot of silver-leaf mirrors and huge chandeliers. Take plenty of money and make your cocktails last— custom-made dense, long-lasting ice cubes help. *Langham Hotel, 1c Portland Pl.* ☎ *020/7636-1000. artesian-bar.co.uk. Tube: Oxford Circus. Map p 124.*

★ Bar Kick SHOREDITCH

Every bar needs to stand out from the crowd. Bar Kick's theme is, appropriately, kicking things. The interior has plentiful table football. TVs show live soccer matches and other sports. *127 Shoreditch High St.* ☎ *020/7739-8700. barkicklondon. com. Overground: Shoreditch High St. Map p 126.*

★ BBar VICTORIA

This bar with South African–inspired decor serves all kinds of cocktails—classic, creative, mocktail, and showstopping vapor cocktails. There's a good wine cellar, strong on South African labels, and a fusion menu of appetizing nosh. *43 Buckingham Palace Rd.* ☎ *020/7958-7000. bbarlondon. com. Tube: Victoria. Map p 128.*

★★★ Blue Bar KNIGHTSBRIDGE

In the lovely Berkeley Hotel, this

The Blue Bar at The Berkeley.

Cocktail garnished with rose petals at The Connaught Bar.

tiny (50-person) and, yes, blue (Luytens Blue, to be exact) bar serves more than 100 varieties of whisky/whiskey, refined cocktails, and tapas-type snacks to a very upscale crowd. No reservations. *Wilton Place.* ☎ *020/7235-6000. theberkeley.co.uk. Tube: Hyde Park Corner. Map p 128.*

★★ **Calloh Callay** SHOREDITCH This long-running bar is very Shoreditch, with just-so wacky touches—gramophone punch bowls, a wardrobe linking the two bars, crazy mismatched decor—attracting a young crowd with adventurous cocktails. The name is derived from *Jabberwocky,* the Lewis Carroll nonsense poem, in case you were wondering. *65 Rivington St.* ☎ *020/7739-4781. calloohcallaybar.com. Tube: Old St. Map p 126.*

★★ **Cecilia's Wine House** COVENT GARDEN Relaxed, brick-walled wine bar with plenty from a European-focused list available by the glass—although value and choice skyrocket if you buy a bottle to share (from £30). Convenient for a pre-theater aperitif,

Cecilia's also serves sharing plates of cheese and cold cuts. *42 Drury Ln.* ☎ *020/7240-9822. ceciliaswinehouse.com. Tube: Covent Garden or Holborn. Map p 124.*

★★★ **The Connaught Bar** MAYFAIR Where guests at this most traditional of hotels go to let off a little steam in fin-de-siècle surrounds. Immaculate service and mixology, with added theater provided by the Martini Trolley. Dress smart-casual. *Carlos Pl.* ☎ *020/7314-3411. the-connaught.co.uk. Tube: Bond St. Map p 124.*

★★ **Craft Beer Co.** COVENT GARDEN Local minichain (8 venues so far) that delivers exactly what you expect: a long line of pumps, fridges heaving with small-batch bottles, and a friendly crowd of beer geeks. *168 High Holborn.* ☎ *020/7240-0431. thecraftbeerco.com. Tube: Covent Garden. Map p 124.*

★★★ **Gordon's** COVENT GARDEN Gordon's first began serving drinks back in 1890, and if the decor has changed since then it's news to us. This gloomy, subterranean place is an absolute institution, with a monthly rotating modern list that usually showcases European and natural wines. Other bars may be swankier, but few can compete for atmosphere. *47 Villiers St.* ☎ *020/7930-1408. gordonswinebar.com. Tube: Embankment. Map p 124.*

★★ **Near & Far Bar** CAMDEN Laid-back cocktails, Palm Springs décor, and a roof terrace in the heart of Camden's nightlife zone. And there's more: casual food and bottomless brunch, with everything 100% gluten-free. *48 Chalk Farm Rd.* ☎ *020/3983-7250. nearandfarlondon.com/camden. Tube: Chalk Farm. Map p 123.*

★★ **The Rake** BANKSIDE Just around the corner from Borough

Tippling in the cellars at Gordon's.

Market, this tiny bar serves, by way of contrast, one of the capital's most diverse selections of independent cask and keg beers. There are often more than 100, way more than there ever are people. There's an equally small garden. *14 Winchester Walk.* ☎ *020/7407-0557.*

www.utobeer.co.uk/the-rake. Tube: London Bridge. Map p 126.

★★ **Sky Garden** THE CITY You have a choice of two bars amid the greenery on top of London's best-nicknamed skyscraper, the "Walkie-Talkie." Expect classic, seasonal, and zero-alcohol cocktails, sharing

Enjoying the sunset from Sky Garden.

The Troubadour.

platters, and a stunning view through massive picture windows. You can just come up here for the view, but you must prebook. *Fenchurch St.* ☎ *0333/772-0020. sky garden.london. Tube: Monument.*

★★ **Spiritland** KING'S CROSS An audiophile's dream of a bar: The whole place is the inside of a bespoke sound system, with speakers everywhere. Cocktails and beers aren't bad, either. *9–10 Stable St.* ☎ *020/3319-0050. spiritland.com. Tube: King's Cross. Map p 123.*

★★ **Troubadour** EARL'S COURT Yes, it's a restaurant, but it's also a wine bar, a jazz club, and a bohemian hangout. Its warren of small rooms holds poetry readings, live music, and singer-songwriter nights. *265 Old Brompton Rd.* ☎ *020/7341-6333. troubadourlondon.com. Tube: Earl's Court.*

★★ **Untitled** DALSTON Small, minimalist interior and Japanese-style garden for inventive cocktails and Asian small plates to nibble.

Reservations highly recommended. *538 Kingsland Rd.* ☎ *07841/022-7924. untitled-bar.com. Overground: Dalston Junction.*

★ **Waxy O'Connor's** SOHO This roaring Irish bar features mad Gaelic music, tipsy crowds, and a shameless sort of tourist appeal. The weird decor improves with each drink—you'll love the indoor tree. Soccer, rugby, and Gaelic sports are shown live. *14–16 Rupert St.* ☎ *020/7287-0255. waxyoconnors london.co.uk. Tube: Leicester Sq. Map p 124.*

Dance Clubs

★★ **Corsica Studios** ELEPHANT & CASTLE Underground sounds in industrial arches below a railway line. The music booms out all night on weekends. *4–5 Elephant St.* ☎ *020/7703-4760. corsicastudios. com. Tickets £5–£25. Tube: Elephant & Castle. Map p 126.*

★★★ **Fabric** CLERKENWELL A legend among Europe's committed weekend partygoers and hot-off-the-press vinyl lovers. Dance till daylight to drum & bass, electro, and techno beats on the "bodysonic" dancefloor, where you can feel the vibrations through your feet. Friday to Sunday only. *77a Charterhouse St. fabriclondon.com. Tickets £11–£30 (book ahead for cheapest prices). Tube: Farringdon. Map p 126.*

★★ **Heaven** COVENT GARDEN Home to G-A-Y (Thurs–Sat)—since the Astoria was demolished to build the Tube's Elizabeth Line—this landmark LGBT-friendly venue, with more than 40 years of partying under its belt, is growing old disgracefully. Live-music gigs midweek. *Under the Arches, Villiers St. ☎ 0844/847-2351. g-a-yandheaven.com. Tickets £5–£25. Tube: Embankment. Map p 124.*

★★ **Ministry of Sound** ELEPHANT & CASTLE This legendary venue has seen competitors come and go over more than 30 years, but is still going strong with multiple bars, huge dance floors, and a hefty Dolby sound system playing techno, hip-hop, house, grime, and garage. Book tickets ahead to ensure entry. *103 Gaunt St. ☎ 020/7740-8600. ministryof sound.com. Tickets £10–£30. Tube: Elephant & Castle. Map p 126.*

★★ **The Social** WEST END Civilized and unpretentious, this bar/club hosts a casual, eclectic, mixed-age crowd, including the occasional celeb. It's tiny, but there's an evening jukebox, live music, and late-night DJs. *5 Little Portland St. ☎ 07939/651-255. thesocial.com. Tickets free–£15. Tube: Oxford Circus. Map p 125.*

★ **XOYO** SHOREDITCH This former print works is a place for dancing, not chilling, laying on a mix of DJ sets and live music. Up to 800 (generally young) revelers gyrate

South of the River

Two decades of investment in urban rail lines has brought many overlooked neighborhoods south of the center within easy reach—and well worth a detour for some fun. The **Bermondsey Beer Mile** (Tube: Bermondsey or London Bridge) is a place of near-pilgrimage for craft beer lovers. There's no official route between the 20 or so bars and brewery taps, but it roughly follows the train line southeast from London Bridge to Bermondsey, with most bars strung along Druid Street and Enid Street. Here you'll find iconic London craft brewer, **The Kernel ★★★** (Arch 11, Dockley Rd. Industrial Estate; thekernelbrewery.com/tap), **Anspach & Hobday ★★** (118 Druid St.; anspachandhobday.com/the-arch-house), and a whole lot more.

At the southern end of the Overground line—marked on Tube maps in lurid orange—the area around Peckham Rye Station is a lively arts, music, and nightlife hub, centered on the **Bussey Building** (copelandpark.com) and **Peckham Levels** (peckhamlevels. org)—both of which have buzzing summer rooftop bars—and the bars and coffeehouses of **Blenheim Grove,** directly below the station platforms.

A show at the O2 Arena.

away in industrial confines. *32–37 Cowper St.* ☎ *020/7608-2878. xoyo. co.uk. Tickets £5–£20. Tube: Old St. Map p 126.*

Live Music

★★★ **KOKO** CAMDEN   You could encounter anything from guitar bands to big-name DJs to an acoustic singer-songwriter at this multistory Victorian theater reborn after a disastrous 2020 fire. Midweek there's an anything-goes music policy; Friday and Saturday are KOKO Electronic club nights. *1A Camden High St.* ☎ *020/7388-3222. koko.co.uk. Tickets £10–£30. Tube: Mornington Crescent. Map p 123.*

★★ **Lafayette** KING'S CROSS Shiny new live music venue in a basement space under the massive King's Cross development. Sharp acoustics suit everything from RnB to alt-country and electro. *11 Goods Way. lafayettelondon.com. Tickets £10–£30. Tube: King's Cross. Map p 123.*

★★ **The Lexington** KING'S CROSS   Grungy pub with a renowned bourbon and rye whiskey list downstairs. Upstairs is a tight-packed stage area for offbeat live acts in almost any genre, plus weekend rock, pop, and 80s club nights. *96–98 Pentonville Rd.* ☎ *020/7837-5371. thelexington. co.uk. Tickets £7–£15. Tube: King's Cross or Angel. Map p 123.*

★ **O2 Arena** GREENWICH   The cavernous interior of the Millennium Dome is now the highest-profile entertainment arena in Britain. Slightly soulless, perhaps, but it's the only place to catch global megastars. Alongside a 20,000-seat main venue is the smaller **indigo at The O2**. *Peninsula Sq. theo2.co.uk. Tickets £2–£150. Tube: North Greenwich.*

★★★ **Ronnie Scott's** SOHO Open since 1959, the granddaddy of London jazz clubs fully deserves its legendary reputation. The best jazz musicians in the world play this classy but relaxed venue every night. *47 Frith St.* ☎ *020/7439-0747. ronniescotts.co.uk. Tickets £10–£55. Tube: Leicester Sq. Map p 124.*

Cheap & Daring: Pub Theaters

In the 1970s a new form of alternative arts venue swept London: the pub theater. Often just an upstairs room where you can bring your beer from the bar, your typical pub theater is where some of the city's most affordable, idiosyncratic, let's-try-this-and-see-if-it-sticks stuff is found—which is why these fringe venues launched many fine actors and incubate West End shows. Four fantastic ones, all mostly charging £20 or less, are the **Etcetera Theatre ★★**, 265 Camden High St. (etceteratheatrecamden.com), a small black box showcasing odd, challenging fare; **Hen & Chickens ★★**, 109 St. Paul's Rd. (henandchickens.com), home to the Unrestricted View company, known for strong writing; **King's Head Pub Theatre ★★**, 115 Upper St. (☎ **020/7226-8561;** kingsheadtheatre.com), whose alums include Kenneth Branagh, Juliet Stevenson, and Hugh Grant in younger, poorer days, and which now focuses on LGBT theater; and **Old Red Lion ★★**, 418 St. John St. (oldredliontheatre.co.uk), a pubby 60-seat space that hosts aspiring producers. Most pub theaters also offer a few comedy nights.

—Jason Cochran, Editor in Chief, Frommers.com

★★★ The Roundhouse

CAMDEN   Homegrown indie talent, transatlantic guitar bands like The National, experimental urban sounds, poetry slam, and even a bit of baroque opera play at an old train shed whose first headline act, in 1966, was Pink Floyd. (And, yes, it's round.) *Chalk Farm Road.* round house.org.uk. Tickets £5–£35. Tube: Chalk Farm. Map p 123.

Wynton Marsalis at Ronnie Scott's.

Pubs

★★ Admiral Codrington

CHELSEA "The Cod" has modern British pub grub, a well-heeled crowd, and a nice atmosphere, made all the better on summer days by a retractable glass roof and outdoor tables. *17 Mossop St.* ☎ *020/7581-0005. theadmiral codrington.co.uk. Tube: S. Kensington. Map p 128.*

★★ Admiral Duncan SOHO

This long-running mainstay of the London gay scene offers bargain shots, cabaret, and drag shows. LGBT or not, it's a fun and friendly place to drink. *54 Old Compton St.* ☎ *020/7437-5300. admiral-duncan. co.uk. Tube: Leicester Sq. Map p 124.*

★★ The Audley MAYFAIR This

is one of London's more beautiful old-school pubs, evocative of a Victorian-era gentlemen's club (it was built in the 1880s). Slip into a booth beneath the original chandeliers for a pint and traditional English grub. *41 Mount St.* ☎ *020/3840-9862.*

theaudleypublichouse.com. Tube: Green Park or Bond St. Map p 124.

★ Cittie of Yorke BLOOMSBURY

There's been a pub on this site since 1430, and although the current building dates back "only" to the 1890s there's still a (faux) old-world vibe and (real) ale at below-average prices. Check out the churchlike interior and its immense wine vats. *22 High Holborn.* ☎ *020/ 7242-7670. Tube: Chancery Lane. Map p 124.*

★★ Coach & Horses SOHO

Refreshingly no-nonsense, unpretentious pub, a throwback to a time before Soho became fashionable. It has bags of character and a traditional singalong with a pianist once a month. *29 Greek St.* ☎ *020/7437-5920. coachandhorsessoho.pub. Tube: Leicester Sq. or Tottenham Court Rd. Map p 124.*

★★★ The Counting House

THE CITY A former bank, this must-see pub has an opulent interior with a glass dome, a balcony

The Audley Public House.

(great for people-watching), extravagant chandeliers, gilded mirrors, and marbled walls. It's busy after work hours. *50 Cornhill.* ☎ *020/7283-7123. the-countinghouse.com. Tube: Bank. Map p 126.*

★★ **The Grenadier** BELGRAVIA This charming pub, tucked away in a secluded mews, is best known for its Bloody Marys, resident ghost, and military past (the Duke of Wellington's soldiers used it as their mess hall). *18 Wilton Row.* ☎ *020/ 7235-3074. grenadierbelgravia.com. Tube: Knightsbridge. Map p 128.*

★★★ **The Harp** COVENT GARDEN This small pub off Trafalgar Square is usually packed to the rafters after work hours—justly so, because it was (and still is) a pioneer of "real ale" and craft beers long before they were cool. Comfy seats upstairs are delightful on a quiet midafternoon. *47 Chandos Pl.* ☎ *020/7836-0291. harp coventgarden.com. Tube: Charing Cross. Map p 124.*

★★ **The Lamb** BLOOMSBURY You'll find one of the city's few remaining "snob screens"—used to protect drinkers from prying eyes—at this Victorian pub. Those who've enjoyed the anonymity here include the Bloomsbury Group and Charles Dickens. *94 Lamb's Conduit St.* ☎ *020/7405-0713. thelamblondon. com. Tube: Russell Sq. Map p 124.*

★★ **The Lyric** SOHO Around 30 taps of cask ales and keg beers draw a chatty crowd to this quaint Victorian pub. Hearty pub classics are served in an upstairs dining room. *37 Great Windmill St.* ☎ *020/ 7434-0604. lyricsoho.co.uk. Tube: Piccadilly Circus. Map p 124.*

★ **Museum Tavern** BLOOMSBURY The early–18th-century Dog & Duck changed its name when the British Museum was built across the street in the 1760s. Old-style décor and etched glass remain mostly intact. *49 Great Russell St.* ☎ *020/ 7242-8987. Tube: Russell Sq. Map p 124.*

★★ **Nags Head** BELGRAVIA This rarity, an independently owned pub, was built in the early 19th century for the posh area's workers. A "no phones" rule attempts to keep the 21st century from intruding. Beers by Suffolk brewery Adnams. *53 Kinnerton St.* ☎ *020/7235-1135. Tube: Knightsbridge. Map p 128.*

★★ **The Toucan** SOHO London's best Guinness? Enough people seem to agree—and even after 30 years' diligent research, I can't say otherwise. *19 Carlisle St.* ☎ *020/7437-4123. thetoucansoho.co.uk. Tube: Tottenham Court Rd. Map p 124.*

★★ **Williamson's Tavern** THE CITY With a history that goes back to Londinium (excavated Roman tiles decorate the fireplace), this pub lies in an alley fronted by gates that were gifts of William III and Mary II. Closed on weekends. *1 Groveland Court.* ☎ *020/7248-5750. Tube: Mansion House. Map p 126.*

★★★ **Ye Olde Mitre Tavern** CLERKENWELL Good service, beamed ceilings, and the stump of a tree Queen Elizabeth I reportedly frolicked under make this historic, hard-to-find treasure a must-see. Closed weekends. *Ely Court, off Ely Place.* ☎ *020/7405-4751. yeold mitreholborn.co.uk. Tube: Chancery Lane. Map p 126.*

Fleet Street Pub Crawl

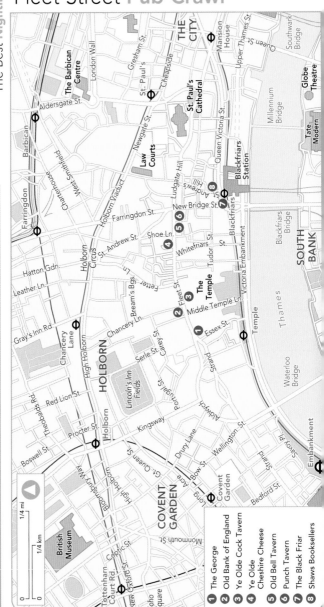

THE CITY

Mansion House

Queen St.

Upper Thames St.

Southwark Bridge

Globe Theatre

Gresham St.

London Wall

The Barbican Centre

Aldersgate St.

St. Paul's

Cheapside

St. Paul's Cathedral

Queen Victoria St.

Millennium Bridge

Tate Modern

Barbican

West Smithfield

Charterhouse

Newgate St.

Law Courts

Ludgate Hill

Blackfriars Station

St. Andrew's Hill

Farringdon

Holborn Viaduct

Farringdon St.

New Bridge St.

Blackfriars

Blackfriars Bridge

SOUTH BANK

Hatton Gdn.

Holborn Circus

St. Andrew St.

Shoe Ln.

Whitefriars

Tudor St.

Victoria Embankment

Thames

Leather Ln.

Fetter Ln.

Bream's Bgs.

Fleet St.

The Temple

Middle Temple Ln.

Gray's Inn Rd.

Chancery Lane

High Holborn

Chancery Ln.

Serle St.

Carey St.

HOLBORN

Lincoln's Inn Fields

Essex St.

Strand

Temple

Waterloo Bridge

Red Lion St.

Theobalds Rd.

Portugal St.

Kingsway

Aldwych

Savoy Pl.

Embankment

Boswell St.

Procter St.

Holborn

Wellington St.

Drury Lane

Bow St.

Long Acre

Strand

Bedford St.

Bloomsbury Way

Gt. Queen St.

High Holborn

COVENT GARDEN

Covent Garden

British Museum

Coptic St.

New Oxford St.

Tottenham Court Rd.

Soho Square

Monmouth St.

1/4 mi

1/4 km

1. The George
2. Old Bank of England
3. Ye Olde Cock Tavern
4. Ye Olde Cheshire Cheese
5. Old Bell Tavern
6. Punch Tavern
7. The Black Friar
8. Shaws Booksellers

If London is, as is often claimed, less a single, cohesive city than a collection of villages, then its pubs are the souls of those villages. "The local" is a place to wind down after work, hang out with friends, gossip, and of course, get rip-roaring drunk. This jaunt explores some of the best watering holes around Fleet Street, once the heart of the U.K. newspaper industry, where every pub was a hotbed of rumor—and source of a potential scoop for any sharp-eared reporter sober enough to remember the morning after.
START: **Tube to Temple.**

Old Bank of England.

❶ ★★ **The George.** Just across from the Royal Courts of Justice, this was a coffeehouse when it opened in 1723 and was frequented by scribblers Horace Walpole, Oliver Goldsmith, and the ubiquitous Dr. Samuel Johnson. A pub since Victorian times, it still has beautiful (if faux) medieval timbering and leaded glass. *213 Strand.* ☎ *020/7353-9638. georgeinthe strand.com. Map p 138.*

❷ ★★ **Old Bank of England.** This unusual pub is housed in a converted former bank branch that retains all the majesty of a palace of finance, with a huge interior and wonderful murals. *194 Fleet St.* ☎ *020/7430-2255. oldbankof england.com. Map p 138.*

❸ ★ **Ye Olde Cock Tavern.** The main reasons to come are its architecture and some former customers: The cockerel was supposedly made by master carver Grinling Gibbons; much of the building survived the Great Fire of London and dates back to the 16th century. It was a favorite of Dickens, Samuel Pepys, and Alfred Lord Tennyson (who mentioned it in one of his poems, a copy of which hangs near the entrance). Closed Sunday. *22 Fleet St.* ☎ *020/7353-8570. Map p 138.*

❹ ★★★ **Ye Olde Cheshire Cheese.** This wonderfully atmospheric, labyrinthine old pub was rebuilt right after the fire of 1666 and hasn't changed much since. Dr. Samuel Johnson lived around the corner, and other literary ghosts haunt the place. It's operated by Samuel Smith's Brewery, whose pints are probably the cheapest in the capital. This is also a decent spot to take on carbs, perhaps a steak or vegetarian pie served with mash. *Wine Office Court, 145 Fleet St.* ☎ *020/7353-6170. ye-olde-cheshire-cheese.co.uk. Map p 138.*

❺ ★★ **Old Bell Tavern.** This cozy and authentic pub was built in the 1670s for workmen building nearby St. Bride's (the "wedding

Points on Pints

Pubs have been the beating heart of British life for centuries. Your neighborhood hangout is known as your **"local,"** but many of the oldest premises have been so well-loved (or well-bombed) that original features are at least partly gone. Most pubs serve food of some kind (snacks, a burger, pies, and the like) for at least part of the day. It commonly costs around £6 for a pint, which in the U.K. is about 20 ounces, 20% larger than a U.S. pint. ABV is typically around 5%, although most pubs now offer at least one zero-alcohol beer. A good **cask ale** is one specialty you should try. Cask ale is not refrigerated or carbonated but stored in the cellar where the temperature is just right for fermentation to continue until the drink hits your glass, having been pulled there by hand. All good pubs have at least a couple of cask ales on offer. For the widest choice, look for **"freehouse"** displayed outside: These pubs are not tied commercially to a specific brewery and may offer drinks from wherever they choose. And remember: When the bell is rung, it's last orders—perhaps as early as 11pm—and the landlord will turf you out.

—Jason Cochran, Editor-in-Chief, Frommers.com

cake" church designed by Wren in 1670). It maintains an old-world ambience with its leaded windows and wainscoted walls. The pub's laidback, genial atmosphere makes it a good spot for a pint or some locally distilled gin. Closed Sunday. *95 Fleet St.* ☎ *020/7583-0216. Map p 138.*

❻ ★★ **Punch Tavern.** Bearing the scars of an ownership feud that divided its premises in two, this Victorian pub (a former gin palace) was where the satirical magazine *Punch* was founded in 1841; look for artifacts from that publication (as well as "Punch & Judy" themed memorabilia) on the walls. The bright interior features beautifully etched mirrors and Art Nouveau chandeliers. *99 Fleet St.* ☎ *020/7353-6658. punchtavern.com. Map p 138.*

❼ ★★★ **The Black Friar.** The amazingly detailed interior of this wedge-shaped Arts & Crafts pub is a feast for the eyes. Magnificent carved friezes of monks remind you that the pub was built on the site of a 13th-century Dominican monastery, and under the vaulted ceiling you'll find such inscribed thoughts as WISDOM IS RARE. It's a popular after-work watering hole with lawyers from nearby legal chambers. *174 Queen Victoria St.* ☎ *020/7236-5474. Map p 138.*

❽ ★ **Shaws Booksellers.** As much a wine bar and restaurant as a pub, Shaws performs each role well. It's set in a restored paper merchant's warehouse, with an elegant, curved-glass bay frontage. Expect upmarket besuited clientele, beers by Fuller's, and a respectable wine list. Closed weekends. *31–34 St. Andrew's Hill. Queen Victoria St.* ☎ *020/7489-7999. shawsbooksellers. co.uk. Map p 138.* ●

Arts & Entertainment Best Bets

Best for a **Laugh**
★★★ The Comedy Store,
1a Oxendon St. (p 147)

Best for **Opera**
★★★ Royal Opera House,
Covent Garden (p 146)

Best **Baroque Concerts**
★★ St. Martin-in-the-Fields
Candlelight Concerts, *Trafalgar Sq.
(p 147)*

Most **Historic Concert Venue**
★★★ Royal Albert Hall,
Kensington Gore (p 146)

Best for a **Horror Movie
All-Nighter**
★★ Prince Charles Cinema,
7 Leicester Pl. (p 148)

Best **Free Live Music
Performances**
★★ LSO St. Luke's, *161 Old St.
(p 146)*

Best for **Independent Cinema**
★ Curzon Mayfair, *38 Curzon St.
(p 148)*

Longest-**Running Show on
the Planet**
★★ The Mousetrap, *St. Martin's
Theatre, West St.*

Best **Classical Acoustics**
★★ Wigmore Hall, *36 Wigmore St.
(p 147)*

Best **Outdoor Performances**
★★ Open Air Theatre, *Inner Circle,
Regent's Park (p 149)*

Above: The magnificent London Coliseum.
Previous page: Albert Sessions, an Evening with Alison Balsom at Royal Albert Hall.

Best for **Ballet**
★★★ Sadler's Wells, *Rosebery Ave.* (p 148); or ★★★ Royal Opera House, *Covent Garden* (p 146)

Best **Orchestra**
★★★ London Symphony Orchestra at the Barbican Centre, *Silk St.* (p 146)

Best for **Modern Dance**
★★ The Place, *17 Duke's Rd.* (p 147)

Best for **New Playwrights**
★★ Royal Court Theatre, *Sloane Sq.* (p 150)

Best for **Shakespeare**
★★★ Shakespeare's Globe, *21 New Globe Walk* (p 150)

Best **Theatrical Repertory Company**
★★★ National Theatre, *South Bank* (p 149)

Longest-**Running Musical in the West End**
★★ Les Misérables, *Sondheim Theatre, Shaftesbury Ave.*

Best **Christmas Pantomime**
★★ Hackney Empire, *291 Mare St.* (p 149)

London **Arts & Entertainment**

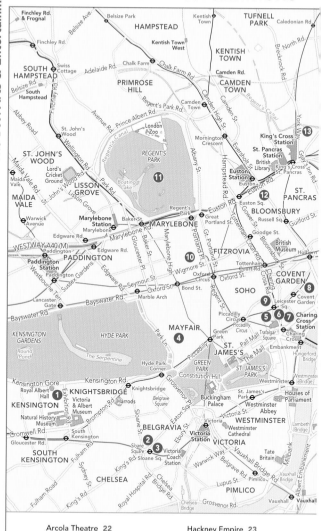

Arcola Theatre **22**
Barbican Centre **18**
The Bill Murray **21**
Cadogan Hall **2**
The Comedy Store **5**
Curzon Mayfair **4**

Hackney Empire **23**
King's Place **13**
London Coliseum **6**
LSO St. Luke's **19**
National Theatre **15**
Old Vic **16**

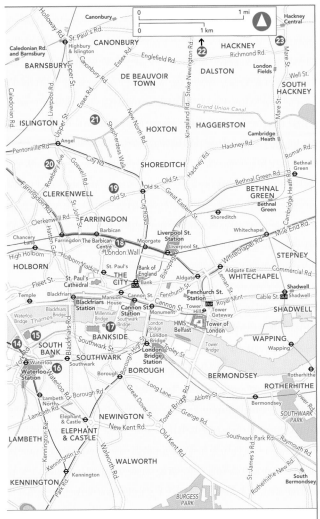

Open Air Theatre 11
The Place 12
Prince Charles Cinema 9
Royal Albert Hall 1
Royal Court Theatre 3
Royal Festival Hall 14

Royal Opera House 8
Sadler's Wells 20
St. Martin-in-the-Fields 7
Shakespeare's Globe Theatre 17
Wigmore Hall 10

London A&E A to Z

Classical, Opera & Multiuse Venues

★★★ Barbican Centre THE CITY

The Barbican's acoustics make it one of London's best places to hear music. The gargantuan 1980s venue is home to the first-class **London Symphony Orchestra** and regularly hosts international ensembles. Dance, theater, indie cinema, and art shows complete the schedule. *Silk St.* ☎ *020/7870-2500. barbican. org.uk. Tickets £10–£70. Tube: Barbican. Map p 144.*

★★ Cadogan Hall CHELSEA

Home to the **Royal Philharmonic Orchestra**, this plush 950-seat venue fills out its eclectic program with touring regional and international companies, musicals, and unplugged contemporary music. *5 Sloane Terrace.* ☎ *020/7730-4500. cadoganhall.com. Tickets £15–£49. Tube: Sloane Sq. Map p 144.*

★★ King's Place KING'S CROSS

Part of the giant redevelopment around King's Cross Station, the home of the **Aurora Orchestra** and regular host of the **London Sinfonietta** offers precise acoustics—don't be rustling any candy wrappers unless you want a row-full of dirty looks. Jazz, world music, and dance performances, too. *90 York Way.* ☎ *020/7520-1440. kings place.co.uk. Tickets £8.50–£70. Tube: King's Cross. Map p 144.*

★★ London Coliseum COVENT

GARDEN   Converted to an opera house in 1968, London's largest theater is home (for now) to the **English National Opera**. Productions range from Puccini to Gilbert and Sullivan to challenging modern fare, all sung in English. Under-21s go free. *St. Martin's Ln.* ☎ *020/7845-9300. eno.org. Tickets £15–£180. Tube: Charing Cross or Leicester Square. Map p 144.*

★★ LSO St. Luke's THE CITY

Designed by Hawksmoor, this deconsecrated church provides an alternative 370-seat venue for the **London Symphony Orchestra** (when it's not at the Barbican). They put on regular free Friday lunchtime concerts. *161 Old St.* ☎ *020/7490-3939. lso.co.uk. Tickets free–£65. Tube: Old St. Map p 144.*

★★★ Royal Albert Hall

KENSINGTON   This splendid Victorian pleasure palace is best known as the home of the annual **Henry Wood Promenade Concerts (The Proms)** in summer, when you'll hear first-rate orchestral classics and chamber music. Pop and rock, often nostalgic reunions, are staged at other times. *Kensington Gore.* ☎ *020/7589-8212. royalalbert hall.com. Tickets £24–£125. Tube: High St. Kensington. Map p 144.*

★★★ Royal Festival Hall

SOUTH BANK   More than 150,000 hours of music have been performed at this acoustically exceptional complex since it opened in 1951. The hall's many free and low-priced concerts make it a great bet for travelers on a budget. *Belvedere Rd.* ☎ *020/3879-9555. southbank centre.co.uk. Tickets £15–£65. Tube: Waterloo. Map p 144.*

★★★ Royal Opera House

COVENT GARDEN   Operas at this historic theater are sung in the original language by first-rate

Crypt. *Trafalgar Sq.* ☎ *020/7766-1100. stmartin-in-the-fields.org. Tickets £9–£32. Tube: Charing Cross. Map p 144.*

★★ Wigmore Hall MARYLEBONE Bechstein Pianos built this grand Renaissance-style recital hall—one of the world's finest—in 1901. The greatest names in classical music have taken advantage of its fabulous acoustics. *36 Wigmore St.* ☎ *020/7935-2141. wigmore-hall. org.uk. Tickets £16–£50. Tube: Bond St. Map p 144.*

Comedy
★★ The Bill Murray ANGEL A mix of the edgy and experimental with work-in-progress sets from the newest and the biggest names in Brit comedy. Good-value shows run almost every evening. *39 Queen's Head St. angelcomedy.co.uk. Tickets £5–£15. Tube: Angel. Map p 144.*

★★★ The Comedy Store WEST END In a previous incarnation, this club launched the alternative-comedy boom of the 1980s. It's still very much a venue where up-and-coming comics aspire to perform and draws the biggest names from the U.K. and international comedy circuit. *1a Oxendon St.* ☎ *020/7024-2060. the comedystore.co.uk. Tickets £15–£25. Tube: Piccadilly Circus. Map p 144.*

Dance
★★ The Place BLOOMSBURY Dedicated to both teaching and performing dance, this small venue is the place in London to see contemporary new artists and startling modern dance. *17 Duke's Rd.* ☎ *020/7121-1100. theplace.org.uk. Tickets £12–£18. Tube: Euston. Map p 144.*

Candlelight concert at St. Martin-in-the-Fields.

international casts. Get online on ticket release date to grab the cheapest seats; each week's Friday Rush (1pm sharp) sees affordable seats released online for every performance over the following 7 days, even sell-outs. Regular free Friday recitals and Monday tea dances (£20) are staged in the magnificent bar. *Covent Garden.* ☎ *020/7304-4000. roh.org.uk. Tickets £12–£285. Tube: Covent Garden. Map p 144.*

★★ St. Martin-in-the-Fields COVENT GARDEN You are following (allegedly) in Mozart's footsteps when you attend a concert at this atmospheric church. Admission to popular lunchtime concerts (Fri 1pm) includes lunch in the Crypt (p 115) for £20. Evening standouts are candlelight classical in the church and jazz or blues in the

Milonga at Sadler's Wells.

★★★ Royal Opera House

COVENT GARDEN   The brilliantly restored 19th-century ROH houses the even more brilliant **Royal Ballet,** a company on a par with the world's best. You can catch any number of classics, such as *Swan Lake, Giselle,* or *Sleeping Beauty,* but you'll pay for the privilege. *See p 146.*

★★★ Sadler's Wells ANGEL

The best dance troupes in the world—from cutting edge to classical ballet—perform across two stages at this chic theatre, where they are assured of a knowledgeable audience. *Rosebery Ave.* ☎ *020/7863-8000. sadlerswells.com. Tickets £15–£85. Tube: Angel. Map p 144.*

Movies

★ Curzon Mayfair MAYFAIR

This historic arthouse theater (dating back to 1934) is renowned for world cinema screenings. *38 Curzon St. curzon.com. Tickets £15–£21. Tube: Green Park. Map p 144.*

★★ Prince Charles Cinema

SOHO   For one of London's quirkiest movie nights, get a ticket for a musical singalong session, 35mm cult hit screening, vintage classic, all-night marathon, or iconic foreign flick. *7 Leicester Pl.* ☎ *020/7494-3654. princecharlescinema.com. Tickets £11–£17. Tube: Leicester Sq. Map p 144.*

Theater

Most high-profile, well-advertised shows play at one of 40-ish West End theaters—mainly located around Shaftesbury Avenue, Leicester Square, Strand, and St. Martin's Lane. This section recommends venues to also seek out for top-quality and/or less mainstream theater.

★★ **Arcola Theatre** DALSTON
Edgy new plays and remastered classics, plus reinterpreted (and new) opera at the summer Grimeborn festival, attract a liberal East London crowd. *24 Ashwin St.* ☎ *020/7503-1646. arcolatheatre.com. Tickets £12–£30. Overground: Dalston Junction or Dalston Kingsland. Map p 144.*

★★ kids **Hackney Empire**
HACKNEY   Touring shows, often with a family flavor, Caribbean-infused comedy, and one of London's best-loved Christmas pantomimes staged in a grand old Edwardian playhouse. *291 Mare St.* ☎ *020/8985-2424. hackneyempire. co.uk. Tickets £10–£45. Overground: Hackney Central. Map p 144.*

★★★ **National Theatre** SOUTH BANK   Home to one of the world's great companies, the National presents the finest in classic drama, award-winning new plays, and musicals, across multiple stages with A-list casts. *South Bank.* ☎ *020/3989-5455. nationaltheatre.org.uk. Tickets £10–£150. Tube: Waterloo or Embankment. Map p 144.*

★★ **Old Vic** SOUTH BANK
Except for a few wartime interruptions, this venerable theatre has been in continuous operation since 1818. The repertory troupe at "the actors' theatre" has been a who's who of thespians over the years, including Sir Laurence Olivier and Dame Maggie Smith. *The Cut.* ☎ *0344/871-7628. oldvictheatre. com. Tickets £13–£85. Tube: Waterloo. Map p 144.*

★★ **Open Air Theatre** CAMDEN
The setting is idyllic, and the seating and acoustics are excellent at

Buying Tickets

The question of when, exactly, to pounce for the cheapest seat is not easy to answer. If you are happy just to experience the West End, the biggest discounts are for same-day performances bought via **TKTS,** the official, nonprofit Society of London Theatre reseller. Their booth on the south side of Leicester Square opens at 10:30am (noon on Sun) or hop online to **tkts.co.uk**. Smash new shows will be hard to get, but good seats at other productions (especially long-running ones) can be 50% off (or even lower). You can find cheap tickets farther ahead via **lovetheatre.com**—but again, don't expect wall-to-wall discounts.

If you have your heart set on seeing a specific hit, visit the theater's website: You'll pay full price, plus a booking fee of up to £4 per ticket. Some concierges can get last-minute tickets to hot shows but you'll be expected to give a 10% tip. Failing that, many theaters sell returns at their box office an hour before curtain.

Twickets (twickets.live) enables theater- and concert-goers to resell their unwanted tickets ethically, at or below face value. You can set up alerts for something specific. Live-music focused **Dice** (dice.fm) offers smartphone ticketing plus an automated in-app waitlist for returns.

Harvest Festival performance at London's Globe Theater.

this Regent's Park venue. Presentations are often of Shakespeare's plays, musicals, or family-friendly shows. Its season runs from mid-May to mid-September. *Inner Circle, Regent's Park.* ☎ *0333/400-3562. openairtheatre.com. Tickets £25–£65. Tube: Baker St. Map p 144.*

★★ Royal Court Theatre

CHELSEA This leader in provocative, cutting-edge theater was founded to promote serious drama and support fresh playwriting—and still does both adeptly. *Sloane Sq.* ☎ *020/7565-5000. royalcourt theatre.com. Tickets £12–£49. Tube: Sloane Sq. Map p 144.*

★★ Shakespeare's Globe

BANKSIDE This outdoor theater is a replica of the Elizabethan original. You can choose to sit on wooden benches (rent a cushion) or stand in front of the stage as a "groundling," just as theater-goers did in the Bard's day. A limited number of £5 groundling tickets are released online every Friday at 11am. *21 New Globe Walk, Bankside.* ☎ *020/ 7401-9919. shakespearesglobe.com. Tickets £5–£10 groundlings, £25–£65 gallery seats. Tube: London Bridge. Map p 144.* ●

9 The Best Hotels

Hotel Best Bets

Best for an **Olde England Vibe**
★★★ Batty Langley's,
12 Folgate St., E1 (p 160)

Best **Hotel for Families**
★★★ Haymarket Hotel,
1 Suffolk Place, SW1 (p 162); or
★★ Park Plaza County Hall,
1 Addington St., SE1 (p 164)

Best **Budget Hotel in
the Center**
★★★ Luna Simone, *47–49
Belgrave Rd., SW1 (p 163)*; or
★★ Cherry Court, *23 Hugh St.,
SW1 (p 160)*

Best **Hotel for Victoriana**
★★ The Gore, *190 Queen's Gate,
SW7 (p 162)*

Best **Hotel for Clubbers**
★★ The Hoxton, *81 Gt. Eastern
St., EC2 (p 163)*

Best **Luxury Hotel**
★★★ Claridge's, *Brook St., W1
(p 160)*

Best **Hotel for Royal Watchers**
★★ The Rubens at the Palace, *39
Buckingham Palace Rd., SW1 (p 164)*

Best **Base for Kensington
Museum-Hopping**
★★ Number Sixteen, *16 Sumner
Pl., SW7 (p 163)*

Best for **Views of the Thames
without Breaking the Bank**
citizenM Tower of London,
40 Trinity Sq., EC3 (p 161)

Best **Bedrooms in East London**
★★★ Town Hall Hotel, *Patriot Sq.,
E2 (p 166)*

Best **Hotel for Afternoon Tea**
★★★ The Goring, *Beeston Pl.,
SW1 (p 162)*

Best **Value for Money**
★★ The Abbey, *20 Pembridge
Gardens, W2 (p 160)*; or ★★ Mama
Shelter, *437 Hackney Rd., E2 (p 163)*

Most **Romantic Hotel**
★★★ San Domenico House,
29–31 Draycott Pl., SW3 (p 165)

Best **Budget Chain**
hub by Premier Inn *(p 161)*

Best **Boutique Chain**
citizenM *(p 161)*

Best **Business Hotel**
★★ St. Pancras Renaissance,
Euston Rd., NW1 (p 164); or
★★ The Zetter, *86–88
Clerkenwell Rd., EC1 (p 166)*

Best for **Theater Buffs**
★★★ Covent Garden Hotel,
10 Monmouth St., WC2 (p 161)

Most **Upscale Atmosphere**
★★★ The Connaught, *Carlos Pl.,
W1 (p 160)*

Best **Rooms Above a Pub**
★★ The Counting House,
50 Cornhill, EC3 (p 161)

Previous page: Handsome guest accommodations at The Hazlitt.

East End & City Hotels

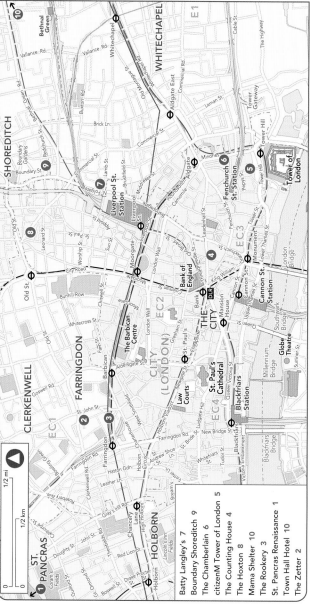

Batty Langley's 7
Boundary Shoreditch 9
The Chamberlain 6
citizenM Tower of London 5
The Counting House 4
The Hoxton 8
Mama Shelter 10
The Rookery 3
St. Pancras Renaissance 1
Town Hall Hotel 10
The Zetter 2

Kensington & Chelsea Hotels

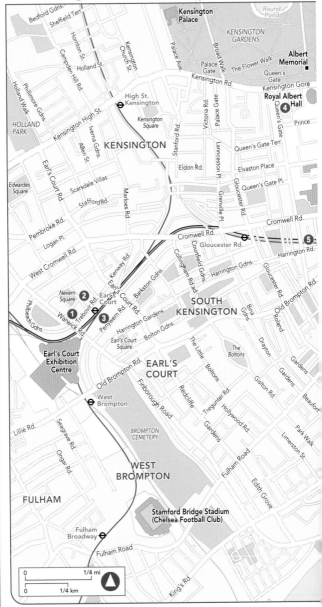

Bedford Gdns.
Sheffield Terr.
Hornton St.
Campden Hill Rd.
Holland St.
Kensington Church St.

Kensington Palace

Round Pond

KENSINGTON GARDENS

Palace Ave.
Broad Walk
The Flower Walk
Albert Memorial

Phillimore Gdns.
Holland Walk

HOLLAND PARK

Kensington High St.
Ivena Gdns.
Allen St.
Stafford Rd.
Scarsdale Villas

Palace Gate
Kensington Rd.
Queen's Gate
Kensington Gore

Royal Albert Hall ❹

Prince

Earl's Court Rd.

High St. Kensington ⊖

Kensington Square

KENSINGTON

Stanford Rd.

Victoria Rd.
Palace Gate
Lanncaston Pl.

Queen's Gate Terr.

Queen's Gate

Eldon Rd.
Elvaston Place

Queen's Gate Pl.

Edwardes Square

Marloes Rd.
Grenville Pl.
Gloucester Rd.

Cromwell Rd.

Pembroke Rd.
Logan Pl.

West Cromwell Rd.

Cromwell Rd.
Gloucester Rd. ⊖ ❺

Collingham Gdns.
Courtfield Rd.
Harrington Gdns.

Gloucester Rd.
Old Brompton Rd.
Harrington Rd.

Nevern Square ❷
Kenway Rd.
Trebovir Rd. ❶
Warwick Rd.
Earl's Court ⊖
❸
Penywern Rd.
Earl's Court Rd.
Barkston Gdns.

SOUTH KENSINGTON

Bina Gdns.
Roland
Drayton

Philbeach Gdns.

Harrington Gardens
Earl's Court Square
Bolton Gdns.

The Little Boltons

The Boltons

Gardens
Gardens
Beaufort

Earl's Court Exhibition Centre

Old Brompton Rd.
EARL'S COURT

Finborough Road

Redcliffe Gardens
Tregunter Rd.
Hollywood Rd.
Gilston Rd.

Park Walk
Limerston St.

West Brompton ⊖

Lillie Rd.
Seagrave Rd.
Ongar Rd.

BROMPTON CEMETERY

WEST BROMPTON

Fulham Road
Edith Grove

FULHAM

Stamford Bridge Stadium (Chelsea Football Club)

Fulham Broadway ⊖
Fulham Road

King's Rd.

0 — 1/4 mi
0 — 1/4 km

Notting Hill & Marylebone Hotels

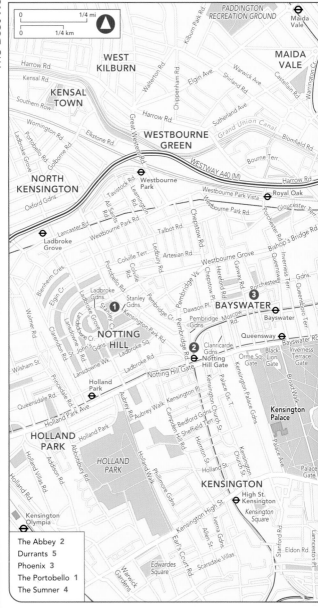

0	1/4 mi
0	1/4 km

PADDINGTON
RECREATION GROUND

Maida
Vale

MAIDA
VALE

WEST
KILBURN

Harrow Rd.

Kensal Rd.

KENSAL
TOWN

Southern Row

Wornington Rd.

Elkstone Rd.

Harrow Rd.

WESTBOURNE
GREEN

Grand Union Canal

Blomfield Rd.

Bourne Terr.

NORTH
KENSINGTON

Oxford Gdns.

WESTWAY A40 (M)

Westbourne
Park

Westbourne Park Vista

Royal Oak

Harrow Rd.

Westbourne Park Rd.

Gloucester Terr.

Ladbroke
Grove

Lancaster Rd.

Westbourne Park Rd.

Talbot Rd.

Chepstow Rd.

Bishop's Bridge Rd.

Colville Terr.

Artesian Rd.

Westbourne Grove

Galway Rd.

Queensway

Inverness Terr.

Queensboro Terr.

Blenheim Cres.

Elgin Cr.

Portobello Rd.

Colville Rd.

Ledbury Rd.

Pembridge Vs.

Chepstow Rd.

Hereford Rd.

Porchester Gdns.

BAYSWATER ❸

Bayswater

Walmer Rd.

Ladbroke Gdns.

Stanley Gdns.

Pembridge Cr.

Pembridge Rd.

Dawson Pl.

Pembridge Gdns.

Moscow Rd.

Queensway

Bayswater Rd.

Inverness
Terrace
Gate

❶

Stanley Cr.

Kensington Park Rd.

NOTTING
HILL

Ladbroke Gro.

Lansdowne Cr.

St. John's Gdns.

Lansdowne Rd.

Ladbroke Sq.

Ladbroke Rd.

❷ Clanricarde
Gdns.

Notting
Hill Gate

Orme Sq.
Gate

Black
Lion
Gate

Broad Walk

Wilsham St.

Lansdowne Wk.

Notting Hill Gate

Kensington Pl.

Kensington Church St.

Kensington Palace Gdns.

Queensdale Rd.

Princedale Rd.

Holland
Park

Aubrey Rd.

Aubrey Walk

Kensington Pl.

Campden Hill Rd.

Bedford Gdns.

Sheffield Terr.

Hornton St.

Kensington
Palace

Holland Park Ave.

HOLLAND
PARK

Holland Park

Abbotsbury Rd.

HOLLAND
PARK

Holland Walk

Phillimore Gdns.

Holland St.

Palace Ave.

Palace
Gate

Holland Villas Rd.

Addison Rd.

KENSINGTON

Kensington
Church St.

High St.
Kensington

Holland Rd.

Kensington
Olympia

Kensington High St.

Iverna Gdns.

Kensington
Square

Allen St.

Scarsdale Villas

Stanford Rd.

Eldon Rd.

Warwick
Gardens

Edwardes
Square

Earl's Court Rd.

Lancaston Pl.

The Abbey **2**
Durrants **5**
Phoenix **3**
The Portobello **1**
The Sumner **4**

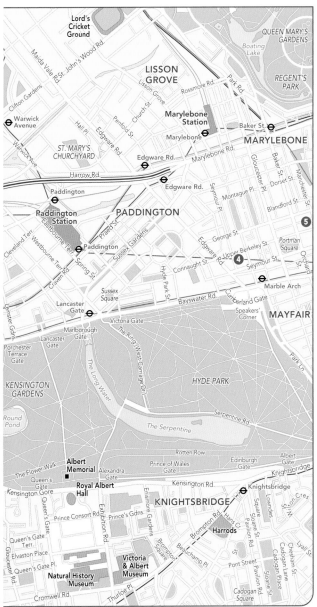

West End & South Bank Hotels

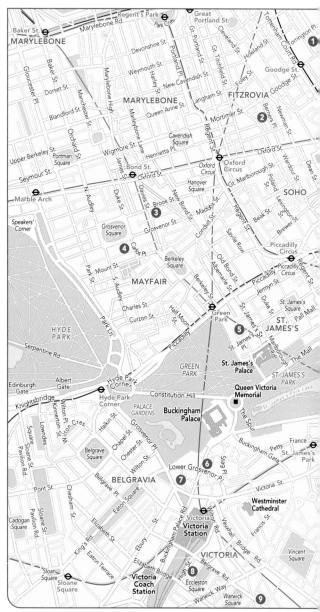

Baker St.
MARYLEBONE
Regent's Park
Park Cres.
Great Portland St.
Marylebone Rd.
Tottenham Court Rd.
Torrington Pl.
1

Baker St.
Gloucester Pl.
Devonshire St.
Portland Pl.
Gt. Portland St.
Cleveland St.
Howland St.
Goodge St.
Goodge St.
Weymouth St.
Harley St.
New Cavendish St.
Gt. Titchfield St.
Foley St.
Newman St.
Berners Pl.
Wardour St.

MARYLEBONE
Marylebone High St.
Manchester St.
Dorset St.
Blandford St.
Queen Anne St.
Langham St.
Mortimer St.
FITZROVIA
2
Dean St.

Orchard St.
Upper Berkeley St.
Portman Square
Wigmore St.
Marylebone Lane
Bond St.
Cavendish Square
Henrietta Pl.
Oxford Circus
Oxford St.
Oxford Circus
Gt. Marlborough St.
Poland St.
Berwick St.
SOHO

Portman St.
Seymour St.
Marble Arch
N. Audley
Duke St.
James St.
Oxford St.
Davies St.
Hanover Square
Regent St.
Beak St.
Brewer St.

Speakers' Corner
Grosvenor Square
Brook St.
New Bond St.
Maddox St.
Conduit St.
Savile Row
Old Bond St.
Piccadilly Circus
Piccadilly Circus
Regent St.

Grosvenor St.
Berkeley Square
3
4
Carlos Pl.
MAYFAIR
Mount St.
S. Audley St.
Albemarle St.
Berkeley St.
Jermyn St.
St. James's Square
Pall Mall

HYDE PARK
Park Ln.
Park St.
Charles St.
Curzon St.
Half Moon St.
Piccadilly
Green Park
5
St. James's St.
Duke St.
Marlborough Rd.
ST. JAMES'S
The Mall

Serpentine Rd.
Edinburgh Gate
Albert Gate
Knightsbridge
Hyde Park Corner
Hyde Park Corner
GREEN PARK
Constitution Hill
St. James's Palace
Queen Victoria Memorial
ST. JAMES'S PARK
St. James's Park Lake

Wilton Pl.
Wilton Cres.
Kinnerton St.
Halkin St.
Grosvenor Pl.
Chapel St.
PALACE GARDENS
Buckingham Palace
The Spur
Sloane St.
Lowndes Square
Sloane St.
Pavilion Rd.
Belgrave Square
Chester St.
Wilton St.
Buckingham Gate
Petty France
St. James's Park
6
Pont St.
Belgrave Pl.
BELGRAVIA
Eaton Square
Lower Grosvenor Pl.
Stag Pl.
7
Victoria St.
Westminster Cathedral

Chesham St.
Cadogan Square
Sloane St.
Pavilion Rd.
Elizabeth St.
Ebury St.
King's Rd.
Eaton Terrace
Buckingham Palace Rd.
Victoria
Victoria Station
Vauxhall Bridge Rd.
Francis St.
Vincent Square

Sloane Square
Sloane Square
Elizabeth Bridge
Victoria Coach Station
High St.
VICTORIA
Belgrave Rd.
8
Eccleston Square
Warwick Way
Warwick Square
9

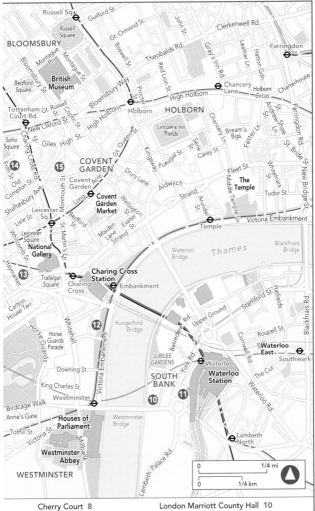

Cherry Court 8
Claridge's 3
The Connaught 4
Covent Garden Hotel 15
The Goring 7
Haymarket Hotel 13
Hazlitt's 14
Jesmond Hotel 1

London Marriott County Hall 10
Luna Simone 9
Park Plaza County Hall 11
The Royal Horseguards 12
The Rubens at the Palace 6
Sanderson London 2
The Stafford London 5

The Best Hotels

London Hotels A to Z

★★ **kids** **The Abbey** NOTTING HILL   Completely renovated in 2022, this four-floor Victorian townhouse has fresh boutique decor, a convenient location close to the Tube, and spacious rooms at great prices—if you can get along without an elevator. *20 Pembridge Gardens, W2.* ☎ *020/3994-5095. theabbeylondon.com. 22 units. Doubles £115–£189. Tube: Notting Hill Gate. Map p 156.*

★★★ Batty Langley's

SPITALFIELDS   A historic 1724 row-house immaculately converted into a luxe Georgian-styled hotel in the shadow of 21st-century skyscrapers. East London's buzzing weekend markets are on the doorstep. *12 Folgate St., E1.* ☎ *020/ 7377-4390. battylangleys.com. 29 units. Doubles £259–£339. Tube: Liverpool St. Map p 153.*

★★ Boundary Shoreditch EAST

END   The opening of this hotel in a converted warehouse was yet another show of confidence in the London visitor's continued push eastward. The airy decor has just the right amount of industrial-chic, plus there's a rooftop bar and grill. *2–4 Boundary St., E2.* ☎ *020/7729-1051. boundary.london. 17 units. Doubles £210–£360. Overground: Shoreditch High St. Map p 153.*

★★ **kids** **The Chamberlain** THE CITY   Business travelers enjoy easy access to the City, and Tower of London sightseers couldn't be happier with the location of this modern hotel above an Edwardian pub owned by London brewer, Fuller's. *132–135 Minories, EC3.* ☎ *020/ 7680-1500. thechamberlainhotel. co.uk. 64 units. Doubles £175–£295. Tube: Tower Hill. Map p 153.*

★★ **kids** **Cherry Court** VICTORIA   They don't come much cheaper than this pleasant hotel, at least not with ensuite facilities and the same degree of cleanliness and comfort. Rooms are small but great value. No elevator. *23 Hugh St., SW1.* ☎ *020/7828-2840. cherrycourthotel. co.uk. 12 units. Doubles £120–£130. Tube: Victoria. Map p 158.*

★★★ Claridge's MAYFAIR   This

Mayfair institution has been the last word in Art Deco elegance for decades. Rooms are spacious, service is impeccable. It's expensive, I know. But it just edges the Connaught (below) as my favorite hotel in London. If you have been saving, or can find a deal, go for it: Claridge's is incredibly special. *Brook St., W1 (at Davies St.).* ☎ *020/7629-8860. claridges.co.uk. 203 units. Doubles £600–£1050. Tube: Bond St. Map p 158.*

★★★ The Connaught MAYFAIR

With all the stately grandeur of a Georgian gentlemen's club, the Connaught is as gloriously dignified as the neighborhood around it. Refurbishment has added modern touches, including contemporary artworks. If you can't afford the steep rates, go for tea (£75) or a

Elegant seating area at Claridge's.

Chain Savings

Faced with rising hotel room rates, cost-conscious travelers increasingly turn to budget brands for an affordable stay. These chains have grabbed the opportunity and massively upped their game, with savvier design, central locations, easy online booking, keen prices, and improved service. On the downside, hotel buildings themselves are often plain and functional, rather than beautiful or "historic." (But then, you don't have to look at them from the inside.)

Premier Inn (premierinn.com) has well-priced hotels with comfy beds in the City, King's Cross, Westminster, and the South Bank, and in trendy Dalston and Brixton. They also run **hub by Premier Inn** (hubhotels.co.uk), pod-style hotels with smaller rooms for one or two, where you control everything with in-room tech. The most important in-room amenities—bed, shower, and Wi-Fi—are topnotch. Their 11 locations include Covent Garden, Soho, Brick Lane, and Tower Bridge.

Travelodge (travelodge.co.uk) has clean, affordable properties in the City, Waterloo, and King's Cross—as well as several outlying boroughs. French-owned **ibis** (ibis.accor.com) has branded hotels close to Borough Market (ibis Blackfriars) and in Greenwich. Fast-growing **Z** (thezhotels.com) has 10+ locations scattered strategically around the tourism zone, from Marylebone to Shoreditch. Rooms are very well equipped but very small (read: You may not have floor space for large suitcases).

Slightly higher in price, contemporary Dutch chain **citizenM** (citizenm.com) offers "no-frills luxury" and XL beds at four convenient locations: Bankside, Shoreditch, Victoria, and Tower of London—a favorite of mine since it opened in 2016, with a cracking rooftop bar. In a similar price bracket, with a business focus, Edinburgh-based **Apex** (apexhotels.co.uk) has a couple of London properties with spacious rooms and luxuries like large showers.

Hand on heart, I would happily stay with any of the above—and have done.

Martini at one of London's best bars (p 130). *Carlos Place, W1.* ☎ *020/7499-7070. the-connaught. co.uk. 123 units. Doubles £400–£680. Tube: Bond St. Map p 158.*

★★ The Counting House THE CITY The floors above one of my favorite City pubs were once a Victorian gentleman's club. Converted to hotel rooms in 2019, they offer sharp, contemporary style and a great location. *50 Cornhill, EC3.*

☎ *020/7283-7123. the-counting-house.com. 15 units. Doubles £200–£314. Tube: Bank. Map p 153.*

★★★ kids Covent Garden Hotel SOHO Big beds, large rooms in multiple configurations, and fresh English interiors by designer Kit Kemp all make this one of the best hotels in the theater district. One downside: The neighborhood gets as noisy at night as it is touristy by day. *10*

The Best Hotels

Monmouth St., WC2. ☎ 020/7806-1011. firmdalehotels.com. 58 units. Doubles £400–£650. Tube: Covent Garden. Map p 158.

★★ kids **Durrants** MARYLEBONE This clubby, family-owned hotel offers good value and a great location close to West End shopping and the Wallace Collection. *32 George St., W1.* ☎ *020/7935-8131. durrantshotel.co.uk. 92 units. Doubles £225–£315. Tube: Bond St. Map p 156.*

★ kids **The Gainsborough** SOUTH KENSINGTON A stone's throw from the Natural History Museum (p 44), this hotel offers basic but comfortable modernized rooms at a budget price. *7–11 Queensberry Place, SW7.* ☎ *020/8159-2773. thegainsboroughhotel. co.uk. 44 units. Doubles £109–£189. Tube: S. Kensington. Map p 154.*

★★ **The Gore** SOUTH KENSINGTON Every room inside this authentic, lavish Victorian hotel is individually decorated with fine antiques. *190 Queen's Gate, SW7.* ☎ *020/7584-6601. gorehotel.co.uk. 50 units. Doubles £200–£340. Tube: Gloucester Rd. Map p 154.*

★★★ **The Goring** BELGRAVIA Although near Victoria Station, this family-owned luxury hotel has the feel of a country house, with a big walled garden, charming public spaces, and refined afternoon teas.

15 Beeston Place, SW1. ☎ *020/7396-9000. thegoring.com. 69 units. Doubles £600–£950. Tube: Victoria. Map p 158.*

★★★ kids **Haymarket Hotel** WEST END The Haymarket's location is perfect for West End fun, and the décor alone is worth dropping by to gawk at. It's not cheap, but neither is putting in a fabulous pool right by Trafalgar Square. Room and good value amenity packages for families if you book direct. *1 Suffolk Place, SW1.* ☎ *020/7470-4000. firmdalehotels.com. 50 units. Doubles £490–£700. Tube: Charing Cross or Piccadilly Circus. Map p 158.*

★★★ **Hazlitt's** SOHO Favored by the literary set, 18th-century-flavored Hazlitt's feels more like a wood-paneled, genteel Georgian boardinghouse than a hotel. There's no elevator. *6 Frith St., W1.* ☎ *020/7434-1771. hazlittshotel.com. 23 units. Doubles £270–£380. Tube: Tottenham Court Rd. Map p 158.*

★★ **Jesmond Hotel** BLOOMSBURY A Frommer's recommendation for decades, this family-owned Georgian townhouse B&B remains the best budget place to stay in Bloomsbury. Two- or 3-night minimum stay; closed Jan. *63 Gower St., WC1.* ☎ *020/7636-3199. jesmond hotel.org.uk. 15 units. Doubles £95–£190. Tube: Goodge St. Map p 158.*

Tudor suite at The Gore.

Groovy bedroom at The Hoxton.

★★ The Hoxton SHOREDITCH
The original Hox is still one of the best, and sits at the heart of the Shoreditch nightlife scene. It does a roaring trade with clubbers who won't (or can't) drag themselves home. Rooms are simple, clean, and well-priced, especially weekdays; the vast, social lobby has a fun vibe. *81 Great Eastern St., EC2.* ☎ *020/7550-1000. thehoxton.com. 210 units. Doubles £169–£350. Overground: Shoreditch High St. Map p 153.*

★★ kids K+K Hotel George Kensington EARL'S COURT   Part of a small European chain, this is a good bet for elegance and convenience at an affordable rate (depending on the season). Enjoy the rare (for London) benefits of private garden. *1–15 Templeton Place, SW5.* ☎ *020/7598-8700. kkhotels. com. 154 units. Doubles £160–£250. Tube: Earl's Court. Map p 154.*

★★ London Marriott County Hall SOUTH BANK   You can't beat the views of Big Ben and Parliament from the rooms, though prices can vary wildly, even day to day. *County Hall, SE1.* ☎ *020/7928-5200. marriott. com. 200 units. Doubles £300–£485. Tube: Waterloo. Map p 158.*

★★★ kids Luna Simone
VICTORIA   Amid a great swamp of cheap accommodation around Victoria Station, the Luna Simone stands head and shoulders above its rivals. The rooms are big enough

for most travelers, everything is neat and tidy, and the staff is supremely friendly. Refurbished in 2018. *47–49 Belgrave Rd., SW1.* ☎ *020/7834-5897. lunasimonehotel. com. 36 units. Doubles £140–£250. Tube: Victoria or Pimlico. Map p 158.*

★★ Mama Shelter EAST END
The Mama ethos has now spread far beyond its Parisian roots. Expect comfy, funky rooms; power-showers; and amenities like a gym. Ideally located for fashion shoppers and night-owls, and a great value on weekdays; less convenient for first-time sightseers. *437 Hackney Rd., E2.* ☎ *020/7613-6500. mamashelter. com/london-shoreditch. 194 units. Doubles £92–£240. Overground: Cambridge Heath. Map p 153.*

★★ kids Mowbray Court EARL'S COURT   This spotless budget hotel features bright, air-conditioned rooms with unshowy furnishings, all refurbished in 2016. Big discounts if you book direct for a multinight stay. *28–32 Penywern Rd., SW5.* ☎ *020/7373-8285. mowbray court.com. 90 units. Doubles £100–£215. Tube: Earl's Court. Map p 154.*

★★ Number Sixteen SOUTH KENSINGTON   This Victorian townhouse hotel with contemporary styling is popular with North Americans and convenient for Kensington's museums. Its quiet orangery and garden are a delight. *16 Sumner Place, SW7.*

Guest accommodations at Number Sixteen.

☎ 020/7589-5232. firmdalehotels.com. 41 units. Doubles £320–£580. Tube: S. Kensington. Map p 154.

★★ kids Park Plaza County Hall SOUTH BANK A wallet-friendly alternative to the Marriott (see above) also in the well-located former County Hall buildings. Rooms are a good size and there are plenty of amenities. Studio Rooms sleep four and have mini-kitchens: A big money-saver for family travelers. 1 Addington St., SE1. ☎ 0333/400-6118. parkplazacountyhall.com. 399 units. Doubles £150–£285. Tube: Waterloo. Map p 158.

★★ kids Phoenix BAYSWATER Unshowy convenience, with a good level of business comfort and decor. Location is the major SP: It's a short walk from both the transport links of Paddington and the open spaces of Hyde Park. 1–8 Kensington Gardens Sq., W2. ☎ 020/7229-2494. phoenixhotel.co.uk. 125 units. Doubles £80–£185. Tube: Bayswater. Map p 156.

★★ The Portobello NOTTING HILL Sumptuously decorated guest rooms are the hallmark of this small, trendy hotel—a longstanding hit with the music and modeling set—located in a discreet Regency terrace near Portobello Road Market. Most rooms no longer have TVs. 22 Stanley Gardens, W11. ☎ 020/7727-2777. portobellohotel.com. 21 units. Doubles £185–£305. Tube: Notting Hill Gate. Map p 156.

★★ kids The Rembrandt SOUTH KENSINGTON This solid tourist hotel across from the V&A (p 32) is popular with travelers for its family deals, location, larger-than-average rooms, and discounted use of a nearby indoor pool and gym. 11 Thurloe Place, SW7. ☎ 020/7589-8100. sarova-rembrandthotel.com. 194 units. Doubles £192–£315. Tube: S. Kensington. Map p 154.

★★ The Rookery THE CITY A sure-footed evocation of 18th-century London, the Rookery is set in design-y Clerkenwell, on the edge of the financial district. Each room is individually decorated with wood panels and antiques. 12 Peter's Lane, Cowcross St., EC1. ☎ 020/7336-0931. rookeryhotel.com. 33 units. Doubles £200–£340. Tube: Farringdon. Map p 153.

★★ kids The Royal Horseguards WESTMINSTER Right in the heart of Royal London, this may be Westminster's best-located hotel. It's less stuffy than you might think—rooms combine modern with traditional chintz—but still makes for a quintessentially English experience at a price lower than you expect. 2 Whitehall Court, SW1. ☎ 020/7523-5062. guoman.com/the-royal-horseguards. 281 units. Doubles £240–£530. Tube: Embankment. Map p 158.

★★ The Rubens at the Palace BELGRAVIA Traditional English hospitality plus the latest creature comforts, just across the road from the Royal Mews. Royal Rooms are slightly more compact but have richer fabrics and the most atmosphere. 39 Buckingham Palace Rd., SW1. ☎ 020/7834-6600. rubenshotel.com. 161 units. Doubles £225–£440. Tube: Victoria. Map p 158.

★★ St. Pancras Renaissance KING's CROSS It's astonishing that this icon of neo-Gothic architecture, designed by Gilbert Scott,

Fine antiques at The Rookery.

was 10 days from demolition in 1967. The old wing is every bit as plush, grand, and historic as you want it to be—and part of Marriott, so flex your points. Proximity to an area transformed this century is another bonus. *Euston Rd., NW1.* ☎ *020/7841-3579. marriott.com. 245 units. Doubles £267–£448. Tube: King's Cross. Map p 153.*

★★ Sanderson London WEST

END If glam is your thing, this is the hotel for you. Inside it's all polished steel, lip-shaped sofas, and Philippe Starck furniture. It has a bit of a party vibe, but refurbished rooms are large, quiet, luxurious, and true to the original Starck vision. The Courtyard Garden is an ideal spot to chill. *50 Berners St., W1.* ☎ *020/7300-1400. sanderson*

london.com. 150 units. Doubles £220–£502. Tube: Goodge St. or Tottenham Court Rd. Map p 158.

★★★ San Domenico House

CHELSEA An exquisite small townhouse hotel that delivers divine Italian period luxury at its most romantic and English-accented. *29–31 Draycott Place, SW3.* ☎ *020/ 7581-5757. sandomenicohouse.com. 19 units. Doubles £239–£435. Tube: Sloane Sq. Map p 154.*

★★ The Stafford London

MAYFAIR This gorgeous 18th-century hotel, spread between three mews buildings in the traditional neighborhood of royal tailors, combines exclusive country style with modern amenities. Look for extended stay deals on their website. *16–18 St. James's Place, SW1.*

St. Pancras Renaissance is set in the famous train station.

Strategies for Staying Outside the Center

There's no sugar-coating it: Central London hotels are pricey. We all love a Thames view or some Mayfair luxe—and among the entries in this chapter, you'll find both, as well as more affordable alternatives. However, to trim the budget, you may also consider a hotel or apartment beyond the center. If so, follow a few rules. Most importantly, **stay near a Tube station:** The Underground is quick from A-to-B, safe, runs until late, and goes almost everywhere. The new Elizabeth Line is the fastest; Piccadilly and Central Lines both bisect the center. Second, **look east:** Lodging in Mayfair or Covent Garden costs twice the price of an equivalent in Shoreditch or Spitalfields. These eastern parts of London have shopping and nightlife that more than matches West London, where budget travelers often huddle. Third, **don't overlook the City**—still very much *in* the center—especially on weekends when business hotels are quieter. It's well connected by Tube and no longer empties out after the working week. Finally, **check the chains** (see "Chain Savings," above), which often do not sell via the usual booking websites.

☎ 020/7493-0111. thestafford london.com. 81 units. Doubles £330–£610. Tube: Green Park. Map p 158.

★★ **The Sumner** MARBLE ARCH One of the West End's few remaining cozy, affordable hotels, the Sumner is a longstanding favorite of clued-in shoppers—and convenient for Hyde Park. 54 Upper Berkeley St., W1. ☎ 020/7723-2244. the sumner.com. 20 units. Doubles £140–£262. Tube: Marble Arch. Map p 156.

★★★ **Town Hall Hotel** EAST END The opening of this place in a 1910 City Hall building further confirmed the East End's status as London's most up-and-coming area. It's as swanky and cool as anything in central London, with Art Deco detailing, a spa and pool, and one of the hottest restaurants around. Patriot Sq., E2. ☎ 020/7871-0460. townhallhotel.com. 98 units. Doubles £170–£315. Tube: Bethnal Green. Map p 153.

★★ kids **Twenty Nevern Square** EARL'S COURT Eclectic Euro–Asian decor, a full range of amenities, and a garden make this one of London's most appealing affordable B&Bs. They also rent three nearby studio apartments. 20 Nevern Sq., SW5. ☎ 020/7565-9555. 20nevernsquare.com. 24 units. Doubles £90–£220. Tube: Earl's Court. Map p 154.

★★ **The Zetter** CLERKENWELL A firm favorite with business travelers in the know, the Zetter is artsy and funky—not formal and dull. The most basic rooms inside this five-story converted warehouse are a little small, but every unit is tastefully done. Those at the top have panoramic skyline views. 86–88 Clerkenwell Rd., EC1. ☎ 020/7324-4567. thezetter.com. 59 units. Doubles £199–£306. Tube: Farringdon. Map p 153. ●

The Savvy Traveler

Before You Go

Tourist Information

Two online-only resources to check before you leave home are Britain's national tourism agency, **Visit Britain** (visitbritain.com), and London's official visitor guide, **Visit London** (visitlondon.com). You can download brochures, as well as Tube, bus, and cycling maps at **visitlondon. com/contact-us**. The **Visit London Official Guide** is also available free from Android and Apple app stores. The website and app are regularly updated with offers, including 2-for-1 ticket deals, the latest exhibitions and arts events, and more ideas.

In London, the only official information bureau with a public office is opposite the south side of St. Paul's Cathedral: The **City Information Centre** (thecityoflfdn.com) sells attraction tickets and Oyster cards, runs good-value walks and tours (cityoflondonguides.com), supplies brochures and walking maps, and offers multilingual travel advice. It's open Monday to Saturday 9:30am to 5:30pm and Sunday 10am to 4pm.

The Best Time to Go

Although prices are highest in spring and summer, the weather is also best then (alas, you should be prepared for showers at any time). Sunny and warm August is a sensible time to visit because that's when many Londoners go on vacation and London's notorious traffic lightens up (very slightly). The only problems? All those extra tourists and, in recent years, heat waves. Fares are cheapest between November and March, Christmas and New Year excepted. The city's museum and theatre scenes are always in full swing, but the winter city can get dark and chilly. September and early October can be gray and rainy, too, but most gardens are still in bloom.

Festivals & Special Events

JANUARY. The **New Year's Day Parade** (☎ 020/3275-0190; lnydp.com) sees an estimated 10,000 performers march, dance, and play their way through London's streets, from Parliament Square to Green Park, to celebrate the start of the year with what may seem to many inappropriate enthusiasm (particularly those still recovering from the night before).

FEBRUARY. **Chinese New Year** (visitlondon.com/china) is celebrated in Soho's Chinatown with dancing lions, red confetti, and street food. The annual **Leadenhall Market Pancake Race** (leadenhallmarket. co.uk/pancake-race) on Shrove Tuesday (called Pancake Day in the U.K.) is a bizarre tradition where teams of runners toss pancakes and try to win the golden pan trophy.

MARCH. One of the month's best-loved events is the **Oxford & Cambridge University Boat Race** from Putney Bridge to Mortlake (theboatrace.org). Pubs and vantage points along the 4-mile route are usually heaving; Hammersmith and Putney bridges are the best places to actually see the boats. Take any chance to crack the age-old joke: "Why is it always the same two teams who reach the final?" March also sees London's large Irish community celebrate **St. Patrick's Day** with floats, musicians, plenty of Guinness, and a nonstop party parade from Hyde Park to Trafalgar Square.

APRIL. Tens of thousands of people compete in the **London Marathon** (tcslondonmarathon.com) every year. The 26-mile course runs from

Greenwich Park to St. James's Park. The best views are from Victoria Embankment.

MAY. A difficult ticket to get hold of, the **Chelsea Flower Show** (rhs.org.uk) is a wonderful spectacle, packed with creative garden displays.

JUNE. The **Royal Academy Summer Exhibition** (royalacademy.org.uk), the world's largest public art display, showcases the works of artists of every genre and caliber. It runs through mid-August. **The Monarch's Official Birthday** (Charles III was actually born in November) is honored with a carriage ride, a gun salute, and **Trooping the Colour** at Horse Guards Parade (householddivision.org.uk/trooping-the-colour). At **London Open Gardens** (londongardenstrust.org), several gardens, usually accessible only to private key-holders, are opened, for one weekend only, to an envious public. **Royal Ascot** (ascot.co.uk/royal-ascot) is the biggest society horse racing event of the year, a time when the upper classes dust off their chapeaus and take part in the old tradition of betting on horses while dressed to the nines and sozzled on Champers. The **All-England Lawn Tennis Championships at Wimbledon** (wimbledon.com) need no introduction, but you will require a hard-to-get ticket (see "Spectator Sports," later in this chapter) or the patience to stand in a long line on the day (or even the preceding evening)—with no guarantee of success.

JULY. The **Proms** (☎ 020/7589-8212; bbc.co.uk/proms), formally the BBC Sir Henry Wood Promenade Concerts, held in and outside the Royal Albert Hall, are the annual joy of London's classical music lovers. The season runs mid-July to early September. **Pride Parades** (pridein london.org) are now held across the country, but the capital's version, on the first or second Saturday in July, is still the biggest event in the LGBT party calendar. The procession heads from Baker Street to Trafalgar Square, and stages are set up around Soho.

AUGUST. The **Notting Hill Carnival** (☎ 020/7221-9700; nhcarnival.org), the largest street festival in Europe, celebrates Anglo–West Indian culture along and around Portobello Road. Expect crowds, beer, music from sound systems and steel bands, and spicy Caribbean cuisine.

SEPTEMBER. During the 2-day **Open House** (open-city.org.uk), hundreds of usually inaccessible architectural gems are opened to the public. For more than a century, at the **Pearly Kings & Queens Harvest Festival** (pearlysociety.co.uk), descendants of London's cockney costermongers (market traders) have dressed in costumes covered with pearly buttons and paraded through the City to a church service at St. Mary-le-Bow Church for charity—and to show off their button-sewing prowess. Floats and carriages make their way from Mansion House to the Royal Courts of Justice and back again during the **Lord Mayor's Show** (lordmayorsshow.london).

NOVEMBER. **Guy Fawkes Night** commemorates the Gunpowder Plot, a thwarted attempt to destroy Parliament in 1605, with bonfires and fireworks all over London. Book a couple of spins on the London Eye (p 13) after dark so you can see London's sky lit up from near and far.

DECEMBER. For show-jumping aficionados, there is no better pre-Christmas fun than the **International Horse Show** (londonshow.com). Tens of thousands of Londoners see in the **New Year** by finding vantage points for the spectacular fireworks display that takes place on and around the London Eye as Big Ben's bongs sound. The closest spots, including Westminster and Waterloo bridges, require a ticket; buy yours online at **london.gov.uk/events**.

The Weather

London's notorious pea-soup fogs have long been eradicated, but a tendency toward showers and gray skies is ever-present—particularly November through February, when the sun shows its face only briefly. The weather can be fickle, and experiencing all four seasons in the span of a single day is common in every season except winter. The general climate is relatively mild, rarely going much above 75°F (24°C) or below 40°F (4°C). Persistent extremes are uncommon, although unpleasant dog days in summer are becoming more frequent: In 2022, new record highs above 104°F/40°C were set—although by the time you read this, they may already have been broken. Snowfall is generally just a day or two during a short, dark midwinter.

For the latest forecast, visit **metoffice.gov.uk**.

Useful Websites & Apps

- **thecityofldn.com**: Official tourism guide to the City, the oldest area of London and now its financial center.

- **royal.uk**: If you're a royal watcher, or just looking for information, trivia, or anything else about the British royal family, direct your browser here.

- **tfl.gov.uk**: London Transport's website is the source of information on London's public transportation system, including the Tube, buses, trains, and ferries.

- **standard.co.uk**: The London *Evening Standard* newspaper's website always has current entertainment and restaurant reviews.

- **timeout.com/london**: Click for cultural event listings, as well as entertainment, restaurants, and nightlife.

- **visitbritain.com**: Great Britain's official tourism website features helpful trip-planning advice.

- **visitlondon.com**: London's official travel website features loads of information and lets you book hotels, buy discount passes, and more.

- **stayinapub.co.uk**: Centuries before London ever had a Hyatt, a local inn was the lodging of choice for the weary traveler. Travel like Dickens or Pepys with the help of this website.

- **Smartify (smartify.org)**: Free official video and audioguides to major London museums including the National Gallery.

- **Bloomberg Connects (bloombergconnects.org)**: Digital guides to major art and culture sites around London, including Sir John Soane's Museum and the Wallace Collection.

Cellphones

If you have a GSM-capable phone, you can make and receive calls in London, although you may accrue whopping roaming charges.

International visitors can buy a pay-as-you-go cellphone (or, if you have an unlocked GSM phone, a SIM-only tariff) at any phone store in London. This gives you a local number and minutes that can be topped up with phone cards or online payments. EE, Three, and Vodafone all offer good service, with 5G coverage across much of the city.

Car Rentals

In a word: Don't. Driving in London is a royal pain and I strongly recommend against it. You're far better on public transportation, when you take into account the daily congestion charge (£15 for entering a large area of the city from 7am–6pm), the dreadful traffic, a dearth of street parking, and the astronomical price of fuel. If you are determined to

LONDON'S AVERAGE TEMPERATURE & RAINFALL					
	JAN	FEB	MAR	APR	MAY	JUNE
Daily High (°F)	46	48	54	59	64	70
Daily High (°C)	8	9	12	15	18	21
Rainfall	2.3/59	1.8/45	1.5/39	1.7/42	1.8/46	1.9/47 (in/mm)

	JULY	AUG	SEPT	OCT	NOV	DEC
Daily High (°F)	75	73	68	61	52	48
Daily High (°C)	24	23	20	16	11	9
Rainfall	1.8/46	2.1/53	2/50	2.6/65	2.6/67	2.4/57 (in/mm)

rent a vehicle, all major car-rental companies operate in the U.K., and cars can be picked up at any London airports.

Getting There

By Plane

Air Canada, American, British Airways, Delta, JetBlue, United, and Virgin Atlantic, among others, offer nonstop service from various locations in the U.S. and Canada to London's major airports. Qantas operates daily service to London from Australian cities including Sydney and Melbourne.

London is served by five airports. **London Heathrow Airport** (heathrow.com), located 15 miles west of London, is the largest. The fastest way into town is the **Heathrow Express** train (heathrowexpress.com) to Paddington Station (15 min.; £25, but up to £19 less if booked online from 90 days in advance; free for children 15 and under). If you don't plan ahead, the walk-up **Tube** fare is a much cheaper option, and with the 2022 opening of the air-conditioned **Elizabeth Line** (40 min.; £13.30), also comfortable. You can take an even cheaper ride on the Tube's Piccadilly Line (1 hr.; £5.60), but it's a grim prospect compared to the Elizabeth Line—and no way to begin your vacation after a red-eye. For either Tube route, pay by **Oyster** (see p 173). Black **taxi cabs** cost roughly £70 to £90 to the city center, depending on traffic and destination. Ride services including **Uber** are allowed to operate at London airports, including Heathrow, but must pick up from designated zones. Traveling into the city by **bus** puts you at the mercy of pretty gruesome traffic. It's not worth the minimal saving.

The city's second airport, **Gatwick** (gatwickairport.com) is 25 miles south of London. The fastest way into the city is on the **Gatwick Express** train (gatwickexpress.com) to Victoria Station (30 min.; £22, £20 online in advance). The slower but cheaper **ThamesLink** train (thameslinkrailway. com; 40–50 min.; £14) is more convenient if you're staying in the eastern part of London: It connects with London Bridge and St. Pancras Stations, and with the Tube's Elizabeth Line at Farringdon. The **bus** into London can take 2 hours and doesn't save you much; check **nationalexpress. com** for a wide network of destinations beyond London. A **taxi ride** to the center usually takes an hour and can cost more than £125.

Stansted (stanstedairport.com) and **Luton** (london-luton.co.uk) airports handle mostly short-hop flights on budget airlines (often easyJet and Ryanair) from European and U.K. destinations. Both are more than 30 miles from London. To get from Stansted to the city, take a **Stansted Express** train (stanstedexpress.com) to Liverpool Street Station (45 min.; £22). From Luton Airport, the most economical method is via **Greenline bus 757** (☎ 0344/800-4411; arrivabus.co.uk/greenline) to Victoria Station (1–1½ hr.; £11.50). **National Express** (nationalexpress.com) operates a similar Luton service. If you're in a hurry, take the train: The **Luton DART** connects every few minutes with a **ThamesLink** service from Luton Airport Parkway to St. Pancras (50 min.; £23).

A fifth airport, **London City** (☎ 020/7646-0000; londoncity airport.com) is by far the smallest and the only one actually in Greater London. It services mainly short-haul jets to business destinations. **DLR** trains run every 8 to 10 minutes to Bank Tube Station (21 min.; £3–£4). A taxi to the center costs around £40 to £50.

By Train

The **Eurostar** provides direct train services between Paris (2¼ hr.) or Brussels (2 hr.) and London's St. Pancras Station next to King's Cross. Make reservations online at **eurostar.com**. King's Cross/St. Pancras has six Tube line connections (Piccadilly, Circle, Hammersmith & City, Metropolitan, Northern, and Victoria), as well as overland trains connecting to the north and Scotland. Buses and taxis are readily available just outside both stations.

National Rail (☎ 03457/48-49-50; nationalrail.co.uk) is the information hub for a plethora of train operators that connect just about every major city in the U.K. to one of London's stations (Charing Cross, Liverpool Street, Paddington, Victoria, King's Cross, Waterloo, London Bridge, and Euston). All major train stations in Central London have Tube stations and offer easy access to buses and taxis.

By Bus

Bus connections to Britain from the Continent, using the Channel Tunnel or ferry services, are generally not very comfortable and take as long as 8 hours, but you can travel to/from Paris for less than £40, if you book well ahead. The long-haul buses of **National Express** (☎ 08717/81-8181; nationalex press.com) traveling within the U.K. and to Continental Europe generally use Victoria Coach Station as their terminus. The bus station is on the corner of Buckingham Palace Road and Elizabeth Street, a few minutes' walk from the main Victoria Station, serviced by Southern, Southeastern, Gatwick Express, and London Underground trains, and a stop on the Underground's District and Circle lines. Victoria has a taxi stand and is the terminus for many city buses. Budget intercity bus operators **Megabus** (uk.megabus.com) and **Flixbus** (flixbus.co.uk) also use Victoria Coach Station.

Getting Around

Discounted Travel

Explaining the prices and passes for London's public transport is a Byzantine exercise worthy of a *Monty Python* skit. Sorting through prices for 1-day and 7-day passes, the rules for different ages of children, prices with and without various discount passes, peak and off-peak travel time, and the different costs of tickets among the outer travel zones in London is complicated. If you want the very latest on pricing and discounted travel, consult the excellent **Transport for London (TfL)** website at **tfl.gov.uk**.

Fortunately, however, you can cut right through all these variables with the efficient and penny-wise **Oyster,** a prepaid, reusable, refillable smartcard that deducts the cost of a trip each time you touch your card to the card reader (white or yellow) found on all public transportation, including trams and buses, the Docklands Light Railway (DLR), Overground rail lines (marked in orange on a map), and regular rail. You pay a one-time charge of £5 for the plastic Oyster smartcard. They can be purchased at any Tube station (including Heathrow Airport stations) or ordered online. It is not necessary to register the card. To retrieve any money left, simply present it at any Tube station and they will refund you on the spot—but you can't get your £5 deposit back. If you're likely to return, keep the Oyster. They never expire.

Apart from convenience, Oyster's major benefit is something called **daily price capping.** No matter how many times you use the card during a 24-hour period from 4:30am through 4:29am the following day, your Oyster automatically calculates the cheapest possible fare. In addition, total charges are capped at a daily maximum that varies according to where exactly you go. For unlimited travel within Zones 1 and 2, you won't pay more than £8.10. The daily cap for Zones 1 to 6 is £15—which includes taking the Elizabeth Line from Heathrow Airport. Even if you mostly walk, paying by Oyster is **much cheaper** than with a paper ticket: A single Tube journey within Zone 1 costs £2.70 with Oyster versus £6.70 with cash.

Alternatively, you can pay for travel with Apple or Google Pay, or a contactless credit or debit card, including American Express. Prices are identical to using the physical Oyster. You swipe your card or smartphone on the reader in the exact same way. Daily caps also apply—which is why most Londoners no longer carry a regular Oyster Card. However, to protect against international banking glitches, unexpected charges, and other hassles, I feel safer recommending Oyster.

You can top up the balance on an Oyster Card at machines (using cash or credit cards) in Underground stations; via the Oyster app; or at any small store displaying the blue Oyster logo in the window or by the checkout.

Under almost every circumstance, **there is no need to buy a 1- or 7-day Travelcard.** Use Oyster instead. It's easier and much cheaper. There are a few outliers and edge cases—if you're traveling in a very large group, for example; in which case, you should check **tfl.gov.uk/fares**.

Tickets for Kids

There are no "family tickets" on London public transportation. However, there are many discounts and lots of free travel available for kids. Children 4 and under travel free everywhere. Up to four children ages 5 to 10 accompanied by a paying adult travel free on bus, Tube, DLR, Overground, some regular rail, and all tram services.

With children ages 11 to 15, ensure their Oyster card has the **Young Visitor discount** activated. TfL and Tube station ticket-window staff can do this free of charge. The Young Visitor discount ensures that your 11 to 15s pay half-fare on pretty much everything, and also have daily fare caps fixed at half the adult rate. The Young Visitor discount remains active for 14 days.

By Underground (Tube)

The world's first subterranean train system (known today as the Underground or **Tube**) was born in London in 1863. Stifling, overpopulated cars, sudden mysterious stops, and arbitrary line closures make the Tube the sacred monster of London's commuters. Love it or loathe it, it's the lifeblood of the city, and its 12 lines (plus the Docklands Light Railway to Greenwich and the London Overground network covering much of eastern and southern suburbia) are usually the quickest way to get from A to B. *Note:* All Tube journeys between two points cost the same whatever route you take. The one exception is the Elizabeth Line from Heathrow into the center, which costs more than double the price of taking the Piccadilly Line.

All Tube stations are clearly marked with a red circle and blue crossbar. Routes are color-coded. The Tube runs daily, except Christmas Day, from around 5:30am to 12:30am (until around 11:30pm Sun), except on Friday and Saturday when a limited **Night Tube** service runs on some lines. At time of writing, services were operating every 10 to 20 minutes through the night on the Jubilee, Victoria, Central, Northern, and Piccadilly lines. On weekends the London Overground through East London, including nightlife hotspots Shoreditch and Dalston, also runs later. For other routes, you must take a night bus or taxi (see below).

Oyster, contactless card, or smartphone travelers should touch the yellow reader to open the gate, and always touch the card as they leave the station (even if there is no gate) or the maximum charge may be applied.

Study a Tube map (available online and at most major Tube stations), or even consult the paper *London A to Z* street atlas (still at many London bookstores), to find the stop nearest your destination. Note that you may have to switch lines to get from one destination to another. The **Citymapper** or TfL Go smartphone apps are indispensable for plotting the most efficient route by Tube, bus, foot, and/or rail. A bonus: 5G mobile service *should* be available on much of the Tube network by 2025.

By Bus

The city's bus system has many advantages over the Tube: With the bus lanes and the (slight) reduction in traffic from the city's congestion, above-ground travel is almost as efficient as the Underground. It also costs about half as much as the Tube for adults—particularly as it's a flat fare right across town—and is completely free for children under 16 (provided they have the appropriate card; see above), offering the potential for big savings for large family groups. And, it has to be said, you get far better views of the city from buses than from Tubes. The city's red double-decker buses are a tourist attraction in their own right. Route maps are available at major Tube stations (Euston, Victoria, and Piccadilly Circus, to name a few) or online at **tfl.gov.uk/maps**.

Fares are a flat-rate £1.75 per adult per journey, regardless of its length, but you **must** pay with an Oyster, contactless card, smartphone, or Travelcard. You touch your card or phone against the reader when you board the bus, but not when you disembark. You can also change buses once within 1 hour without paying extra (you still touch the reader on the second bus, but you won't be charged). Remember to touch your card or phone to one of the card readers on the bus, or you may be fined. Inspectors often board buses to catch fare evaders.

Buses are cashless and there are no single tickets or ticket machines.

A full day of bus fares caps out at £5.25, no matter how many rides you take. Most children ride free; see "Tickets for Kids," above.

Night buses are the only way to get to most of the city by public transport after the Tube stops operating. Be sure there is an "N" bus listed on your bus stop's route or you'll wait in vain until morning.

By Taxi or Ride Service

All airports and train stations have well-marked areas for London's legendary black cabs, many of which are now colored with advertising but still the same distinctive model that holds five people. You can hail a licensed taxi anywhere, on any street, except in certain no-stopping zones marked by red lines along the curb. Available taxis will have the sign on top of the cab

illuminated. Taxis can also be requested by phone or the **Gett** app.

Only black cabs, whose drivers have undergone rigorous training known as "the Knowledge," are allowed to cruise the streets for fares. Don't get into cruising minicabs, which can legally pick up only those passengers who have prebooked. Black cabs have metered fares (the minimum fare is £3.80, though you won't get far for less than £15), and surcharges are assessed after 8pm and on weekends.

If you phone a minicab, check and/or negotiate charges in advance. A popular choice is **Addison Lee** (addisonlee.com), including for fixed-fare airport transfers. Ride service **Uber** also operates and its drivers must be licensed. **Lyft** is not in London.

Fast **Facts**

APARTMENT RENTALS Alongside the usual global names, **SilverDoor Apartments** (☎ 020/8090-8090; silverdoorapartments.com) offers serviced apartments in various city locations. **Onefinestay** (☎ 855/553-4954 in U.S.; onefinestay.com) occupies the luxury end of the market.

ATMS Also known locally as "cashpoints" or "holes in the wall," ATMs are everywhere, and most use global networks such as Cirrus and Plus. Note that you may be charged a fee by your bank for withdrawing pounds from your home currency account. Be aware, however, that contactless card payments are everywhere. Some places don't even accept cash.

BABYSITTING Reputable babysitting agencies with vetted employees include **Sitters** (☎ 03330/032-888; sitters.co.uk) and **Universal**

Aunts (☎ 020/7738-8937; universalaunts.co.uk). Rates are about £11.50 per hour. Hotel guests must usually pay a booking fee and reasonable transportation costs.

BANKING HOURS Most banks are open Monday through Friday from 9am to 5pm; some also have limited Saturday open hours.

BIKE RENTALS Cycling opportunities have increased dramatically since the launch of London's sponsored bike-sharing program, now known as **Santander Cycles.** Anyone can hire a bike from one of hundreds of docking stations dotted across town. You can return the bike to any station, making the rental perfect for short trips. Charges are £1.65 per 30 minutes. Buy access with a payment card at the docking station. For more frequent use, or to access Santander e-bikes (£3.30/30 min.) join online at **santandercycles. tfl.gov.uk**. The official app will help you locate the nearest docking stations. A handful of "dockless" e-bike and e-scooter services also operate, including **Lime** (li.me). **London Bicycle Tour Company,** 74 Kennington Road (☎ **020/7928-6838**; londonbicycle.com) rents a wide variety of bikes, including touring bikes, e-bikes, and kids' bikes. Rates start at £4 per hour and £24 per day (£48 for 3 days). Provision of dedicated cycle lanes all over the center is growing fast, too.

BUSINESS HOURS Stores generally open at 9am and close around 6pm Monday through Saturday, though they may stay open until 8 or 9pm at least 1 night per week (usually Thurs). Sunday opening hours are typically 11am or noon to 5pm, though some places may open longer. Post offices are open 9am to 5:30pm on weekdays; a few also open Saturdays.

CONSULATES & EMBASSIES American Embassy, 33 Nine Elms Ln. (☎ **020/7499-9000**; uk.usembassy. gov). **Canadian High Commission,** Canada House, 1 Trafalgar Sq. (☎ **020/7004-6000**; international. gc.ca). **Australian High Commission,** Australia House, Strand (☎ **020/7379-4334**; uk.embassy. gov.au). **Irish Embassy,** 17 Grosvenor Place (☎ **020/7235-2171**; dfa.ie). **New Zealand High Commission,** 1 Pall Mall E. (☎ **020/ 7930-8422**; mfat.govt.nz).

CUSTOMS Check **gov.uk/bringing-goods-into-uk-personal-use** for what foreign visitors may bring into London. For specifics on what you can bring home with you, check with your home country's customs authority.

DENTISTS Emergency Dentist branches at 102 Baker St. and 9 Artillery Ln. (near Liverpool St. Station; ☎ **020/7486-1047**;

24hour-emergencydentist.co.uk) provide 24-hour emergency dental service.

DINING Breakfasts range from the traditional "full English" of fried eggs, bacon, sausage, beans, grilled tomato, and toast to a more Continental menu of croissants, baguettes, and coffee. If your hotel doesn't include breakfast in its rates, going to a cafe instead will likely be cheaper. Most cafes open from 8am. Most restaurants open for lunch from noon to 3pm, and for dinner from 6 to 10 or 11pm. Dress codes have become much more relaxed; no one will raise an eyebrow at casual clothing except at very expensive restaurants and a few hotel dining rooms. You will encounter general disapproval if you bring small children to the fanciest restaurants, especially at dinnertime.

Many London restaurants take reservations through **OpenTable, Resy,** and other booking apps. You can also ask your hotel's concierge for help when you arrive, or when you call to reserve a room.

DOCTORS A number of on-call doctor services can treat you and dispense medicine at your lodgings, or you can go to them. **Doctorcall,** 121 Harley St. (☎ **0844/257-0345**; doctorcall.co.uk), makes house calls. You can get non-urgent medical advice over the phone by calling ☎ 111. In an emergency; call ☎ 999.

ELECTRICITY Britain uses a 220–240 volt system and alternating current (AC); its electrical plugs have three pins. European appliances will require only a plug adapter, but American 110-volt appliances will need both a transformer and an adapter or they will fry and blow a fuse. Most laptops, phones, and tablets have built-in electrical transformers, but will need an adapter plug.

EMERGENCIES Call ☎ **999** for accidents and dire medical emergencies free of charge from any phone. Hospitals with emergency rooms (known as Accident and Emergency departments, or A&E) in Central London include **University College London Hospital,** 235 Euston Rd. (☎ 020/3456-7890; uclh.nhs.uk), **Chelsea & Westminster Hospital,** 369 Fulham Rd. (☎ **020/3315-8000;** chelseawest.nhs.uk), **St. Mary's Hospital,** Praed St., Paddington (☎ 020/3312-6666; imperial.nhs.uk), and **St. Thomas' Hospital,** Westminster Bridge Rd. (☎ **020/7188-7188;** guysandst thomas.nhs.uk).

EVENT LISTINGS Good sources of event and entertainment listings and reviews include *TimeOut* (time-out.com/london) and the *London Evening Standard* newspaper (standard.co.uk/culture). The **Visit London** website (visitlondon.com) also has a "Things to Do" section.

FAMILY TRAVEL Look for items tagged with a kids icon in this book. Most British hotels accommodate families, and all but the poshest restaurants are usually family-friendly. The vast majority of museums have signage, treasure trails, and activities aimed at various age groups; the latter tend to be most prevalent on weekends and during school holidays. **Visit London** has a section on its website dedicated to families (www.visitlondon.com/things-to-do/family-activities) that provides information on attractions, immersive experiences, and activities, and usually has a few discounts on various goods and services.

HOLIDAYS Bank holidays, on which some shops, museums and all banks, public buildings, and services, are closed, are as follows: New Year's Day, Good Friday (Fri before Easter), Easter Monday, May Day (first Mon in May), Spring Bank Holiday (last Mon in May), August Bank Holiday (last Mon in Aug), Christmas Day, and Boxing Day (Dec 26). These days, only Christmas Day sees near-total retail shutdown. The Tube runs every day except December 25.

INSURANCE Check your existing insurance policies and credit card coverage before buying travel insurance. You may already be covered for lost luggage, canceled tickets, or medical expenses. To find a policy to match your needs, try marketplace sites such as InsureMyTrip.com, Travelinsurance.com, and SquareMouth.com.

INTERNET Free Wi-Fi is omnipresent, including in almost all hotels. Cafe chains **Costa** (costa.co.uk), **Pret** (pret.co.uk), **Caffè Nero** (caffenero.com/uk), and **Starbucks** (starbucks.co.uk) offer free Wi-Fi to customers, as do most indie coffee shops. Almost 350 Tube and Overground stations also have Wi-Fi; 5G mobile coverage is promised across the Tube by 2025.

LGBTQ TRAVELERS London has one of the most active LGBTQ scenes in the world. The **Visit London** website (visitlondon.com) has advice on everything from LGBT-friendly lodging to bars and other entertainment. **PinkNews** (thepinknews.com) is a long-running and respected London source of news and reviews.

LOST PROPERTY Be sure to tell all your credit card companies the minute you discover your wallet has been lost or stolen, and file a report at the nearest police station (your insurance company may require a police report before covering any claims). If you've lost all forms of photo ID, call your consulate and airline and explain the situation. It's always best to keep copies of your credit card numbers and passport information in a separate, secure location in case you lose the real items.

Property lost on London public transport (buses, Tube, Overground, and black taxis) is collected by **TfL;** your first stop should be to follow the instructions on their website at **tfl.gov.uk/help-and-contact/lost-property.** If you've lost something on an overland train, contact the main terminal that serves the train on which you lost your property.

LUGGAGE STORAGE If you are staying in an Airbnb or similar rental, you can store luggage at several places around London. Try searching **Bounce** (usebounce.com) or **Stasher** (stasher.com) for a convenient location. Expect to pay £5 to £6 per bag for up to 24 hours, including insurance. **LuggageHero** (luggagehero.com) can work out cheaper for just an hour or two of storage. Major rail stations usually have a "left luggage" service, too.

MAIL & POSTAGE Stamps for a small letter mailed inside the U.K. cost £1.10 for first class and 75p for second class. Postage for postcards and letters sent International Standard (6–7 days to arrive) from the U.K. to North America costs £2.20. You can pay for and print out postage at **royalmail.com.** The city's distinctive red mailboxes are plentiful. The closest post office to Trafalgar Square and Covent Garden, at 393 Strand, is open from 9am to 6pm Monday to Friday, and 9:30am to 5pm Saturday.

MONEY The U.K. currency is the pound sterling: £1 consists of 100 pence (pennies). There are 1- and 2-pound coins; silvery 50p, 20p, 10p, and 5p coins; and copper 2p and 1p coins. Banknotes are issued in denominations of £50 (red), £20 (lavender), £10 (copper), and £5 (blue). Notes are now made from a polymer that makes them more durable.

Foreign money can be exchanged at most banks and bureaux de change, but you'll be assessed a hefty surcharge or get terrible conversion rates. If you want to arrive with a few pounds in hand, get them at home. ATMs (known locally as "cashpoints") are located all over the city and offer the best exchange rates; find out your daily withdrawal limit before you leave. At the time of writing, £1 was worth $1.27. For the most up-to-date currency conversion information, go to **xe.com**.

A growing number of stores and cafes in London **no longer accept cash.** Payment with smartphone or tap-and-pay card (called "contactless" in the U.K.) is everywhere, even for the smallest purchases; locals often go weeks without using cash. If you're given the choice of paying in the local currency or your own currency, always choose local, as your credit card will always have a better exchange rate than the one local businesses will give you. *Note:* Be sure to notify any card providers before leaving for London, so they don't become suspicious when the card is used overseas and block your account.

PARKING Parking in London is difficult, even for those who have paid for a resident parking permit (yet another reason not to drive here). Metered spaces have time limits of 1 to 4 hours and are hard to find.

Garages (parking lots) are expensive, but a bit more plentiful. Look for signs that read **NCP** (National Car Parks); check **ncp.co.uk/find-a-car-park** for locations, prices, or to prebook. Always check any warning signs on streets for info on temporary parking suspensions. Parking violations are punished with a hefty fine, tire clamping, or the removal of your car to an impound lot. If your car has been towed, visit **met.police.uk/advice** and follow instructions for vehicle recovery. On top of all that, there's the daily congestion charge to pay (see p 170).

To summarize: **Do not drive in London.**

PASSES The **London Pass** (london-pass.com) incorporates free admission to several of London's highest-priced attractions, as well as an open-top bus tour and other useful discounts. Pass package prices are as follows: 1 day £84 adults, £49 children; 3 days £132 adults, £74 children; 6 days £169 adults, £104 children. But remember: You *don't* need the London Pass for most museums because they are free. However, you will save quite a lot of money if you cram high-profile, fee-charging attractions into your time here. For example, it's doable to see the Tower of London, Westminster Abbey, St. Paul's Cathedral, the Painted Hall, Shakespeare's Globe, and Kensington Palace within 3 days. Entry to just those six costs almost £150, versus £132 for those plus much more with the London Pass, including a Roamer ticket for unlimited 1-day use of Thames Clippers boats (another £21). On the other hand, the total cost of admission to the British Museum, Tate Modern, V&A, Natural History Museum, National Gallery, Sir John Soane's Museum, and Wallace Collection is zero. As a rule of thumb, if you like sights and historic buildings, think seriously about the London Pass. If you prefer art and museums, it's unlikely to represent a good value.

Warning: The **London Pass + Travel** option costs more than arranging an Oyster yourself (which is easy; see p 173).

PASSPORTS Citizens of the U.S., Canada, Ireland, Australia, and New Zealand currently need only a valid passport to enter the U.K. However, by 2025, almost everyone entering the U.K. visa-free will need an **Electronic Travel Authorisation (ETA)** before they travel, even babies. Apply online at least a couple of weeks ahead at **gov.uk** or download the UK ETA App. The ETA costs £10 per person.

Always make a copy of your passport's information page and keep it separate from your passport in case of loss or theft. For emergency passport replacement, contact your country's embassy or consulate (see "Consulates & Embassies," on p 176).

PHARMACIES Known here as "chemists," each can fill a valid doctor's prescription. The leading drugstore chain in the U.K., **Boots** (boots.com) has branches all over London. To find a pharmacy close to you—including 24-hour pharmacies—use the search tool at **nhs.uk/service-search/pharmacy**.

SAFETY London has its share of violent crime, just as any other major city does—its biggest crime-related problems are public intoxication and muggings—but it is usually quite safe for visitors, as long as you take common-sense precautions. Good safety tips include:

- Use your hotel safe.
- Be alert when withdrawing money from ATMs; don't take out more cash than you need, and don't carry around large sums.
- Guard your valuables in public places and keep your wallet in an inner pocket. Pickpockets operate in major tourist zones.
- Don't leave pocketbooks dangling from chairs in restaurants or cafes; use a purse that closes securely.
- Avoid conspicuous displays of expensive jewelry.
- Avoid the upper decks of buses late at night. Take a cab if you can afford it.
- Stay alert in high-end shopping areas: Bags from luxury shops are a tip-off to thieves.
- There's safety in numbers—don't wander alone very late at night. And stay out of parks after dark.

- Don't hop in a minicab hailed off the street. Stick to official black cabs (p 175) or licensed services such as Uber.

SENIOR TRAVELERS Discounts (concessions) for seniors 65 and over are often available (with proof of age) for museums and some entertainment.

SMOKING Smoking is prohibited in shops, all public transportation, and all public buildings. It's also forbidden inside restaurants, pubs, and bars (although these may have dedicated outside smoking areas). Tobacco is expensive in the U.K., so if you smoke, bring your cigarettes from home.

SPECTATOR SPORTS London is crazy for football (that's soccer to you North Americans) and is home to several professional teams. One of the best places to watch the English lose their decorum (although tickets are hard to come by) is at **Arsenal Football Club,** Emirates Stadium, Drayton Park (☎ **020/7619-5000;** arsenal.com). Wear red and you'll fit right in. For a more genteel (albeit confusing) experience, try watching a cricket match at the sport's hallowed field, **Lords Cricket Club,** St. John's Wood Rd. (☎ **020/7432-1000;** lords.org).

The most revered annual sporting event is probably June's **All-England Lawn Tennis Championships at Wimbledon** (wimbledon. com). Check the website for details on how to enter your name for the annual ticket lottery. Same-day seats are available, but you'll wait in very long lines—fanatics often queue from the night before.

TAXES A 20% value-added tax (VAT) is included in almost everything you buy, from hotel bills and restaurant checks to most merchandise and services. Price tags on items in stores **must** already include the VAT (except in some antique shops). Gasoline (petrol) in Britain is further taxed via a Fuel Duty, making it very expensive.

TAXIS See "By Taxi or Ride Service," on p 175.

TELEPHONES London's city code is **020,** but you don't need to dial it within city limits from a fixed line; just dial the eight-digit number. To call London from the rest of the U.K., or from anywhere using a mobile phone, you must dial the 020 followed by the number. When calling London from abroad, dial the international code (011 from North America, 0011 from Australia, and 00 from New Zealand), followed by 44 (England's country code), followed by 20, and then the eight-digit number.

When calling abroad from London, dial 00, the country code, the area code, and then the number.

TICKETS Many West End theaters keep a few seats in reserve to sell on the day of a performance. If you're set on seeing a specific show or event (especially the ballet or opera), book tickets well in advance through the venue's box office.

You can get discounted theater tickets from **tkts**—online at **official-londontheatre.com/tkts** or at the kiosk on the south side of Leicester Square—for many shows. The closer to showtime, the bigger the discount (usually). For more information on buying tickets, see p 149.

TIPPING Tipping is much less common in the U.K. than in many other countries (notably the U.S.). It is not usual to tip chambermaids (though you may certainly do so), bartenders in pubs, or taxi drivers—unless they've helped you with your luggage, in which case a 10% tip will suffice. Hairdressers should be tipped 10%. Hotel porters should get £1–£2 per bag; doormen should get £1–£2 for hailing you a cab. Scan any restaurant check for an automatic service charge, which usually runs around 10% to 15%. If service hasn't been included, tip your waiter 10% to 15%, so long as you feel their service merited it. You aren't expected to tip at a pub unless table service is provided.

TOILETS   Clean public toilets can be found in most shopping centers and major railway stations. Some are free, although others charge 50p or even £1 for use. Pubs and hotels don't usually mind if you discreetly nip in to use the loo (especially if you buy a drink first). Department stores have public restrooms, usually stashed on high floors to discourage traffic. For more information on public restrooms (loos), see p 75.

TOURIST OFFICES   Most resource these days goes into maintaining the excellent **visitlondon.com**. The only official walk-in tourism office is the **City Information Centre** opposite the south side of St. Paul's Cathedral (Tube: St. Paul's). It has information in multiple languages, leaflets, maps, and an event ticket booking service, as well as free Wi-Fi. It's open Monday to Saturday from 9:30am to 5:30pm, Sunday 10am to 4pm.

TOURIST TRAPS & SCAMS   Some of the half-price theater-ticket shops around Soho are rip-offs (they tag on a heavy commission for poor seats), and many tickets sold on the street are counterfeit; use only the official **tkts** booth (p 149) at the south end of Leicester Square or official online sellers. For music concerts and other one-off events, it's worth checking for resales via **Twickets** (twickets.live), even at the last minute; don't use street touts. Don't buy anything from street peddlers. See "Safety," above.

TOURS   Two similar companies offer good orientation tours of the city by double-decker bus: **London Big Bus** (bigbustours.com) and **Toot-bus** (tootbus.com). Tickets, good for 24 hours, allow visitors to hop on and off buses that pass sights and stop at major attractions (buses run every 15–30 min. and take 2–3 hours). Both companies charge around £45 adults, £25 for kids 5–15 (10% less online in advance); audio commentary is available in several languages, there's free Wi-Fi, and a river trip is included. Upgraded tickets often adda themed walking tour. Yes, open-top buses can feel a bit *cringe*. And you could piece together the route with your Oyster (p 173) for less than a tenner. But if you're on a mega-tight schedule, they cover some highlights quickly and hassle-free.

Black Taxi Tours of London (☎ 07946/106-939; blacktaxitours.co.uk) offers personalized 2-hour tours in a genuine black cab for up to five people for £165. The cabs can venture where buses cannot, making it easier to get off the tourist trail. You can also choose your own theme, from the Beatles to Harry Potter.

For walking tours of London geared to specific interests, you can't do better than **London Walks** (☎ 020/7624-3978; walks.com). Engaging guides lead visitors on tours ranging from ghost walks to strolls through literary London to movie location tours. Walks cost £15 each. **CityGuides** (cityoflondon-guides.com) specializes in themed walks—Roman London, the Great Fire, and more—around the Square Mile, London's oldest neighborhood. The meeting point is the City Information Centre and you must book by 9pm the day before. Most walks cost £12 per person.

If you want to see London from the Thames, forget the tours and jump on a **Thames Clipper** (thames clippers.com). These river commuter boats run every 20 minutes or so through the center, connecting West London with Westminster, Bankside, Tower Bridge, Canary Wharf, and more with points east. This is the very best way to arrive at **Greenwich** (p 60). It's most economical to buy tickets in the Uber app or tap your Oyster at the dock (p 173). Note, however, river boat fares are **not included in the daily cap** (see above). Fares vary by distance traveled; for example, one-way Westminster to Greenwich costs £9.40 (£12.30 if you buy a physical ticket at the pier). Children ages 5–15 go half-price.

Many museums and royal palaces offer **excellent daily gallery talks** and themed tours inspired by the various objects in their collections. They're often free: Check individual museum websites.

TRAVELERS WITH DISABILITIES Most of London's major museums are fitted with wheelchair ramps, as are almost all buses. Black taxis are all accessible. Discount (or free) admission ticket for travelers with disabilities are offered by many attractions and theaters. **Tourism for All** (tourismforall.org.uk) offers information and advice for travelers with disabilities visiting Britain. Visitors with disabilities planning to travel via public transportation should consult the excellent dedicated section of the **Transport for London** website (tfl.gov.uk/transport-accessibility) for downloadable access maps, guides, and other advice.

VAT See "Taxes," above.

A Brief **History**

A.D. **43** Romans invade England and settle Londinium.

61 Queen Boadicea sacks Londinium in a brutal but unsuccessful rebellion against Rome.

200 Romans fortify the city with a wall.

410 Roman troops abandon London as their Empire falls.

600 King Ethelbert builds first St. Paul's Church on ruins of Temple of Diana.

800 Vikings raid Britain.

885 Alfred the Great captures London from the Vikings.

1042 Edward the Confessor is crowned king of England and begins work on Westminster Abbey.

1066 William the Conqueror is crowned king of England in Westminster Abbey after the Battle of Hastings. London becomes seat of political power.

1078 Construction of the Tower of London begins.

1176–1209 London Bridge is built, the first permanent stone crossing linking the two banks of the Thames.

1192 Henry FitzAilwin is elected first lord mayor of London.

1215 Magna Carta is signed by King John.

1240 First Parliament is convened at Westminster.

1348 First outbreak of the Black Death plagues London.

1381 Wat Tyler's Peasant Revolt is mercilessly crushed.

1476 William Caxton, the first English printer, revolutionizes English printing and makes Fleet Street the country's publishing center.

1599 Shakespeare's first play is performed at the Globe Theatre.

1605 The Gunpowder Plot to destroy Parliament is thwarted on November 5.

1642 The Puritan government orders the closure of playhouses such as the Rose and the Globe.

1649 Charles I is beheaded at Whitehall.

1653 Oliver Cromwell is made Lord Protector of the Realm. Puritan rule closes London's theatres, brothels, and gaming halls.

1665 Outbreak of bubonic plague kills 100,000 Londoners.

1666 Great Fire of London sweeps through the city.

1667 Christopher Wren begins work on St. Paul's Cathedral; attempts to redraw London's layout are abandoned.

1675 The Royal Observatory is founded in Greenwich.

1688 James II is banished during the Glorious Revolution; William and Mary move into Kensington Palace.

1694 First Bank of England is established in the City of London.

1735 Dr. Samuel Johnson moves to London and becomes a fixture on the coffeehouse circuit.

1759 The British Museum is opened to the public.

1810 London's first Indian restaurant opens.

1829 Robert Peel sets up Metropolitan Police force, known as "bobbies" in his honor.

1836 Charles Dickens publishes The Pickwick Papers and becomes London's favorite novelist.

1837 Eighteen-year-old Queen Victoria ascends the throne and moves into Buckingham Palace.

1851 Great Exhibition takes place in Hyde Park, financing the development of South Kensington.

1854 Cholera epidemic in London results in improved sewage system.

1857 Victoria & Albert (V&A) Museum opens.

1860 London's first public flushing toilet opens.

1863 London opens the world's first Underground Transit System (Tube).

1908 For the first time, London hosts the Olympic games at White City.

1909 American Gordon Selfridge opens London's iconic department store.

1914 World War I starts; zeppelins drop bombs on London.

1939–45 World War II air raids kill thousands in London and destroy much of the city's infrastructure.

1948 London hosts the first post-war Olympic Games.

1951 Festival of Britain held on the South Bank.

1953 Queen Elizabeth II is crowned in Westminster Abbey.

1956 The Routemaster red double-decker bus takes to the streets.

1963 Youth-quake in London: The Beatles and the Rolling Stones rule the day.

1981 Prince Charles marries Lady Diana Spencer in St. Paul's Cathedral.

1986 The M25, London's orbital highway, opens.

1994 London is linked to Paris by rail via the Channel Tunnel.

1997 London mourns the death of Princess Diana.

2000 Pigeon feeding in Trafalgar Square is outlawed.

2002 London celebrates Queen Elizabeth II's Golden Jubilee.

2005 London wins bid for the 2012 Olympics; 55 die in July 7 terrorist attacks on London transport.

2008 "Red" Ken Livingstone is ousted as Mayor of London by Boris Johnson.

2012 London hosts the Olympic Games for the third time (the first time with the Paralympic games).

2016 Londoner Sadiq Khan is the first Muslim elected to be mayor of a European capital city.

2018 London enters its second decade hosting regular season NFL games at Wembley Stadium.

2020 Like much of the planet, London falls silent for the COVID-19 pandemic. Streets are empty except for a few, mostly empty red buses.

2023 King Charles III is crowned in a lavish ceremony at Westminster Abbey. The following month, the Cubs and the Cardinals tie the second MLB London series with one win each.

London's **Architecture**

Norman Period: 1066–1200

The oldest-surviving style of architecture in London dates back to the time of William the Conqueror, when Norman invaders from northern France overran England. Thick walls and masonry were used to support the large interiors needed to accommodate the churchgoing masses. The heavy construction usually gave Norman buildings a dark and foreboding air.

Characteristics of the period include:

- Thick walls with small windows
- Round weight-bearing arches
- Huge piers (square stacks of masonry)
- Chevrons—zigzagging decorations surrounding doorways or wrapped around columns

The Tower of London's **White Tower,** built by William the Conqueror, is a textbook example of a Norman-style castle. **St. John's Chapel** within the White Tower is one of the few remaining Norman-style churches in England.

Gothic: 1200–1550

Also French in origin, the fairytale Gothic style introduced engineering innovations that enabled builders to transfer weight away from a structure's walls so they could be taller and thinner. The style also allowed for the use of larger windows, which allowed more natural light to reach a building's interior.

In addition to the pointed arch, Gothic construction features:

- Vaulted ceilings, using cross vaulting (an "X" design) and fan vaulting (a more conic design)
- Flying buttresses, free-standing exterior pillars that helped support the building's weight
- Carved tracery stonework connecting windows
- Stained-glass windows

You need look no further than **Westminster Abbey,** built in the mid-14th century, for a perfect London example of the Gothic style.

Renaissance: 1550–1650

The Renaissance style, involving proportion and mathematical

The Wren Style

One of the great geniuses of his age (and London's greatest architect), Sir Christopher Wren (1632–1723) was a professor of astronomy at Oxford before becoming an architect. After the Great Fire of London in 1666, Wren was chosen to rebuild the devastated city and its many churches, including St. Paul's, on which work began in 1675. His designs had great originality, and he became known for his spatial effects and his impressive fusion of classical and baroque. He believed in classical stability and repose, yet he liked to enliven his churches with baroque whimsy and fantasy. Nothing better represents the Wren style than the facade of St. Paul's (p 12, **❽**), for which he combined classical columns, reminiscent of Greek temples, with baroque decorations and adornments.

precision enlivened by decoration, was imported from the Continent by the great Inigo Jones, who was greatly influenced by Italian Palladianism.

Characteristics of Renaissance architecture include:

- A sense of proportion
- A reliance on symmetry
- The use of classical columns— Doric, Ionic, and Corinthian

Top examples of this style include the **Banqueting Hall at Whitehall** and the **arcade** of Covent Garden, both designed by Inigo Jones.

Baroque: 1650–1750

Baroque architects Christopher Wren and Nicholas Hawksmoor had unrivalled opportunities to practice their craft in London when the Great Fire of 1666 provided a clean palette on which to replace medieval wooden structures.

The prime features of the more fanciful baroque style include:

- Classical forms marked by grand curving lines
- Decoration with playful carvings

St. Paul's Cathedral, with its massive dome and complex exterior decor, is Wren's crowning achievement and the finest example of English baroque architecture in London.

Neoclassical & Greek Revival: 1750–1837

Neoclassicism was an 18th-century reaction to the busy nature of baroque architecture. Notable characteristics of neoclassical architecture include:

- Clean, elegant lines, with balance and symmetry
- Use of classical Greek columns
- Crescent layouts (half-circles of identical stone houses with tall windows)

Sir John Soane's Museum and John Nash's curving white stucco **Cumberland Terrace** in Regent's Park are exemplars of these styles.

Gothic Revival: 1820–1900

As industrialization began its inexorable march on London, artists and architects looked back to a supposedly simpler and more romantic, whimsical period for their inspiration.

The features that marked the Gothic Revival style include:

- A confusion of spires, arches, and decorative detail
- Buildings constructed on a grand scale

The **Palace of Westminster,** home to the British Parliament, is the farthest-reaching exponent of this style; the most compact is the **Albert Memorial** in Hyde Park.

20th & Early 21st Century: 1900–Present

The 20th century saw London expanding into its suburbs with uninspired architecture. The Blitz was the period's (far more tragic)

version of the Great Fire, and rebuilding took place with postwar austerity. The stark utilitarian style of South Bank's **Royal Festival Hall** is in a style known as **Brutalism. Post-modernism** is a softening of that style, applying the whimsy of the past to the modern, which brought about the inside-out **Lloyd's Building** and the **Gherkin Building.** The best marriage of old and new can be seen in the covered **Great Court** of the British Museum, which managed to put a new hat on an old friend without making it look silly.

Useful London Terms & Language

London has one of the world's most famous argots. **Cockney rhyming slang** emerged from the East End during the 19th century and consists of words and phrases constructed using a rhyme—a creative process that makes what you're talking about both less likely to be understood by the uninitiated, and more likely to be humorous. To make the dialect still more obscure, the word that formed the original object of the rhyme is often omitted. For example, "bread" meaning money derives from a rhyme with "bread and honey" and "ruby" meaning curry derives from "Ruby Murray," a 1950s singer. Although some words and phrases have entered common parlance— "barnet," from "Barnet Fair," meaning hair is another—you're unlikely to hear too much pure rhyming slang as you travel the city.

However, London does have a vocabulary of its own—some of it derived from or influenced by Cockney, some disparagingly referred to as "mockney," some

related to products, places, and produce that are peculiar to the city, and some just plain slang. You may also notice the liberal use of the F-word on London's streets. Although it certainly isn't considered a polite word, its impact on the local listener is more diluted than in North American cities.

Below is a glossary of some London words and phrases you may encounter.

bangers sausages; usually paired with mashed potato for "bangers and mash"; also an excellent song, tune, or goal in a soccer match

banging good; often applied to music

barking crazy or mad; coined from a former asylum in the eastern suburb of Barking

barney an argument or disagreement

bedlam madness; as in "the roads are bedlam today"; a corruption of "Bethlehem," an asylum formerly at the corner of Moorgate and London Wall, in the City

black cab an official London black taxi, as opposed to a private hire "minicab" or an Uber; only black cabs are permitted to tout for fares curbside

butcher's a look (from Cockney "butcher's hook"); as in "can I have a butcher's?"

BYO short for "bring your own"; a restaurant that doesn't sell alcoholic drinks but will happily open any you bring along, sometimes for a small corkage fee

circus a (usually circular) coming together of streets, as at Piccadilly Circus and Finsbury Circus

clink a prison; after the former Clink Prison, on the South Bank

damage the cost, check, or bill; as in "what's the damage?"

dodgy not to be trusted, suspect; as in "that £20 note looks dodgy"

dosh money; also "bread" or "dough"

gaff home; "back to my gaff" means "back to my place"; also "manor," derived with a heavy dose of irony from the "country manor" where nobles, squires, and other English gents would frolic

G 'n' T gin and tonic; often served with "ice and a slice," i.e. an ice cube and a lemon wedge

gastrocaff a fashionable cafe that nevertheless serves traditional English fried breakfasts

geezer a man; also "bloke" or "fella"

greasy spoon the opposite of "gastrocaff": a basic cafe known for fried food

IPA India Pale Ale; a type of hoppy, light-colored English bitter ale first brewed in the 18th century; now usually carbonated and heavily hopped in line with U.S. beer styles

lager straw-colored, fizzy light beer such as Budweiser and Foster's, served colder than traditional ales (although it's a myth that English beers are served "warm"; they should appear at cool cellar temperature)

liquor green parsley sauce served in traditional pie and mash shops (see "The Best Dining," p 105)

naff cheap looking, or unfashionable

Porter type of dark, strong ale once popular with London dockers; London brewers Kernel brew a definitive contemporary version

pint both a measure of beer and a generic term for having a drink; as in, "do you fancy going for a pint later?"

quid one pound; "10 quid" or "a tenner" is £10

subway a pedestrian underpass; the underground railway is known as "the Tube"

wally a type of pickled gherkin, often paired with fish and chips

yard see "gaff" but more commonly used by younger Londoners

Index

See also Accommodations and Restaurant indexes, below.

Photo **Credits**